"Preaching is the rudder of the church; it provides direction, clarity, and the raw material the Holy Spirit uses to transform lives. Every honest pastor wants to become a more powerful and effective communicator and Sunukjian's Biblical Preaching for the Contemporary Church series is one of the most effective tools I know. His coaching and example have had a significant role in shaping how I teach God's word today and I highly recommend his work to you."

—**Chip Ingram,** Senior Pastor, Venture Christian Church;
Teaching Pastor, Living on the Edge

"These model sermons remind us that exposition should be interesting, relevant, and at the same time thoroughly biblical. These messages should not just be read by pastors, but by anyone who wants their soul blessed by the transforming truth of the Scriptures."

—**Erwin W. Lutzer,** Senior Pastor, The Moody Church

"We are living in a day when Bible exposition has fallen on hard times. There are too few models and even fewer practitioners. Sunukjian is one of the best at wedding solid biblical exposition with creative and relevant applications. His artful use of imagination and penetrating questions in connecting the listener to the text is an invaluable guide for faithfully preaching the ever true and practical Word of God."

—**Mark L. Bailey,** President and Professor of Bible Exposition,
Dallas Theological Seminary

"Good preaching is both a science and an art. While it is relatively easy to master the science of exegesis, the final product is wrapped in the far more challenging art of application, illustration, and delivery. I've found that being exposed to communicators who do the art well has been both instructional and inspirational. This book is full of outstanding examples of sermons that excel in both science and art. If it is true that great preaching is not only taught, but caught, then reading through these sermons will be a significant help in upgrading the effectiveness of your preaching!"

—**Joseph M. Stowell,** President, Cornerstone University

"Sunukjian is not only an influential teacher of preachers; he's also an outstanding biblical expositor. In his exceptional new Biblical Preaching for the Contemporary Church series, Sunukjian wears both hats and helps his readers become more effective biblical communicators as he demonstrates excellent examples of contemporary expository preaching. His sermons are filled with fascinating illustrations and timely application while also reflecting powerful insights into the biblical text. These are books that will encourage any reader—pastor or layperson—and they deserve a place on any preacher's bookshelf."

—**Michael Duduit**, Executive Editor, *Preaching* magazine;
Dean, College of Christian Studies and the Clamp Divinity School,
Anderson University

"Some things can best be taught; others are better caught than taught. Good preaching requires both, which is why we should all be grateful for the unique combination found in Sunukjian's textbook, *Invitation to Biblical Preaching,* and now his Biblical Preaching for the Contemporary Church series. The instruction and examples provided by this veteran expositor and teacher of expositors are unmatched in their usefulness to preachers everywhere."

—**Duane Litfin**, President Emeritus, Wheaton College

"Much ink has been spilled in recent years on matters homiletical. These works have been mostly theoretical and some exhortative, but hardly any modeling of sermons. Sunukjian has done the church and the pastorate a service with his carefully thought out expository sermons in this series of books. The preacher who has an ear will harken to these examples from the pen of a master preacher and teacher of preachers—well worth the investment of one's time. It will sharpen your skills, spark your creativity, and shape your productions in the pulpit, for the glory of God and the edification of his people."

—**Abraham Kuruvilla,** Professor of Pastoral Ministries,
Dallas Theological Seminary

"The best way to learn how to preach well is to copy the masters. Sunukjian's Biblical Preaching for the Contemporary Church series puts into print a wealth of biblical expositions that are worth imitating. Fulsome, gripping introductions draw the reader into the life issue which the text of Scripture—and therefore the sermon—addresses. Ideas flow logically, just as one would expect from the author of *Invitation to Biblical Preaching*, where Sunukjian demonstrates unparalleled mastery of that skill. The content of each sermon is well-researched but it doesn't sound overly academic. Sermons reflect the preaching portion's contribution to the biblical book being expounded. The oral style is engaging and the illustrations not only clarify ideas, they shed the light of Scripture on us who hear them. These volumes will do preachers who read them a lot of good—so long as they learn from the preacher and resist the temptation to copy his sermons!"

—**Greg R. Scharf,** Professor of Pastoral Theology,
Trinity Evangelical Divinity School

"Nearly everything I learned about sermon preparation and delivery, I learned from my former preaching professor Don Sunukjian. His new series Biblical Preaching for the Contemporary Church is a must-read for every preacher and teacher who desires to effectively communicate God's timeless truths."

—**Robert Jeffress,** Pastor, First Baptist Church, Dallas, Texas

"From my first bite into the meaty-yet-accessible volumes of Sunukjian's Biblical Preaching for the Contemporary Church series, I was taught and touched by its blend of solidity in depth with insight in content, bringing together an enriching immediate practicality."

—**Jack Hayford,** Founder and Chancellor, The King's University

BIBLICAL PREACHING
FOR THE CONTEMPORARY CHURCH

Invitation to Philippians:
  Building a Great Church through Humility

Invitation to James:
  Persevering through Trials to Win the Crown

Invitation to the Life of Jacob:
  Winning through Losing

Invitation to Galatians
  (forthcoming)

Invitation to Mark
  (forthcoming)

Invitation to Joshua
  (forthcoming)

INVITATION TO THE LIFE OF JACOB

WINNING THROUGH LOSING

Donald R. Sunukjian

WEAVER BOOK
COMPANY
WOOSTER, OHIO

Invitation to the Life of Jacob: Winning through Losing
© 2014 by Donald R. Sunukjian

Published by
Weaver Book Company
1190 Summerset Dr.
Wooster, OH 44691
Visit us at weaverbookcompany.com

Cover design: LUCAS Art & Design
Editorial, design, and production:
    { In a Word } www.inawordbooks.com
    /edited by Margaret Diehl/

Library of Congress Cataloging–in–Publication Data
Sunukjian, Donald Robert.
    [Sermons. Selections]
    Invitation to the life of Jacob : winning through losing /
Donald R. Sunukjian.
        pages cm.—(Biblical preaching for the contemporary church)
    ISBN 978-1-941337-10-3
    Kindle ISBN 978-1-941337-17-2
    ePub ISBN 978-1-941337-18-9
1. Jacob (Biblical patriarch)—Sermons. 2. Bible. Genesis xxv–xxxiii—Sermons. I. Title.
    BS580.J3S86 2014
    222'.11092—dc23
                                    2014018318
Printed in the United States of America
14 15 16 17 18/ 5 4 3 2 1

To the faculty and staff at
Talbot School of Theology

I say of the holy people who are in the land,
"They are the noble ones in whom is all my delight."
Psalm 16:3

CONTENTS

SERIES PREFACE

Some years ago I wrote a textbook—*Invitation to Biblical Preaching*—which has been translated into several languages and is being used rather widely to develop biblical preachers. This current series of volumes is being published as an *Invitation* to sermons on specific biblical books, individuals, or themes. The purpose of this series is to offer models of the principles presented in the textbook.

A sermon comes alive when it is true to the biblical author's flow of thought, clear in its unfolding, interesting to listen to, and connected to contemporary life. Hopefully that's true of the messages in this book.

These messages were originally preached before a congregation of God's people, and then slightly edited to their present form in order to adjust from the *hearing ear* to the *reading eye*. But I've tried my best to retain their oral flavor—I've wanted them to still sound close to the way we talk. This means there will be incomplete sentences, colloquial and idiomatic language, and other features of the spoken word.

I've also occasionally included some *stage directions,* so that the reader can visualize any props or large physical movements that were part of a message.

May God speak to your heart through his Word.

INTRODUCTION

A fascinating man with a turbulent life—that's Jacob.

Other than Samson, Jacob was probably the strongest man in the Bible. He lifted from the top of a well a flat rock that three teenage boys could not lift. He physically wrestled God to a draw, in whatever magnificent human form God took for the occasion.

His mind was always active, looking for the edge, the advantage. He manipulated, finessed, and deceived. And then received what he had sown as others did the same to him.

He immigrated penniless to a new country. Within twenty years, he was a multi-millionaire. And along the way he fathered twelve sons who became the Jewish people.

He came into the world with God's irrevocable promise of blessing, but he never could trust God to make good on it.

Even after he seemingly gained a victory, with a new name to reflect it, he soon relapsed into fear and finagling.

Jacob is Everyman. Jacob is us.

1

A TWINKLE IN YOUR PARENTS' EYES
OR A STAR IN GOD'S PLAN

Genesis 25:19–26

"I knew you when you were just a twinkle in your parents' eyes," an older friend of the family sometimes said to a youngster in my family when being introduced. In other words, "I knew your parents even before you were born, when they were just twinkling loving eyes at one another."

Is that simply what your life is? Are you merely the result of a twinkle in your parents' eyes? Or is there some more meaningful reason for your birth, some greater significance to why you're here? Is there some plan of God's in which you play a starring role?

The life of Jacob tells us that the latter is true: God has a plan for your life, and intends to bless you beyond what you expect. Your existence on earth is not an accident; you were a "planned pregnancy." God brought you into the world with a specific purpose and he plans to bless you and use you more than you know.

The question is: How do you receive this blessing? What response will enable you to enjoy his blessing and fulfill his purpose? The answer will emerge as we watch Jacob coming into the world. From the moment of his birth, we'll see that God has a specific plan for him—a plan to bless him and use him. And we'll learn what's necessary to receive that blessing.

Jacob's story begins in Genesis 25:19–26:

> This is the account of the family line of Abraham's son Isaac. Abraham became the father of Isaac, and Isaac was forty years old when he married Rebekah daughter of Bethuel the Aramean from Paddan Aram and sister of Laban the Aramean.

*Isaac prayed to the L*ORD *on behalf of his wife, because she was childless. The L*ORD *answered his prayer, and his wife Rebekah became pregnant. The babies jostled each other within her, and she said, "Why is this happening to me?" So she went to inquire of the L*ORD.

*The L*ORD *said to her,*

> *"Two nations are in your womb,*
> > *and two peoples from within you will be separated;*
> *one people will be stronger than the other,*
> > *and the older will serve the younger."*

When the time came for her to give birth, there were twin boys in her womb. The first to come out was red, and his whole body was like a hairy garment; so they named him Esau. After this, his brother came out, with his hand grasping Esau's heel; so he was named Jacob. Isaac was sixty years old when Rebekah gave birth to them.

The opening line—"This is the account of the family line of Abraham's son Isaac"—immediately connects Jacob to God's specific plan for his life. "This is the account of" is a special phrase in the book of Genesis; it organizes or structures the whole book. Appearing ten times in the book, it reveals God's unfolding plan as he more specifically narrows and focuses on whom he will use to carry out his purposes in the world.

"This is the account of" means "This is what became of so-and-so." It's not so much about the person mentioned as it is about the family line that comes from him—the descendants who follow him, and what happens to them as God dismisses some from blessing and chooses others. Here are the ten occurrences of the phrase in Genesis, with the consequences that follow:

2:4	This is what became of the heavens and the earth—sin enters the world in the Garden.
5:1	This is what became of Adam—sin becomes rampant and universal.
6:9	This is what became of Noah—after a flood destroys a sinful world, God establishes his covenant with Noah's descendants.
10:1	This is what became of Noah's sons—his descendants rebel against God at Babel.

11:10	This is what became of Shem—his descendants lead to Abram, whom God will choose.
11:27	This is what became of Terah—his descendants, Abraham and Isaac, are chosen.
25:12	This is what became of Abraham's son Ishmael—his descendants are dismissed.
25:19	This is what became of Abraham's son Isaac—his descendant Jacob is chosen.
36:1	This is what became of Esau—his descendants are dismissed.
37:2	This is what became of Jacob—his descendants multiply in order to bless the world.

Genesis 25:19, therefore, means: "This is what became of Abraham's son Isaac; this is the descendant of Isaac's who will now become part of God's unfolding plan."

But what is this plan that Jacob is going to be so central to? How specifically does God intend to bless him and use him?

The plan is to give Jacob millions of descendants, descendants who will teach the world about God. Eventually one of these descendants will bring the world to God. God's plan is to multiply Jacob's descendants and use them to reveal God's truth to the world; ultimately, one of these descendants, Jesus Christ, will bless the world by restoring them to God.

This plan was first announced to Jacob's grandfather Abraham—millions of descendants, and eventually one who will bless everyone on earth:

> The LORD had said to Abram, "Go from your country, your people and your father's household to the land I will show you.
> "I will make you into a great nation
>   and I will bless you;
> I will make your name great,
>   and you will be a blessing.
> I will bless those who bless you,
>   and whoever curses you I will curse;
> and all peoples on earth
>   will be blessed through you." (Gen. 12:1–3)

This is the plan and the promise—millions of descendants to bless the world. It begins with Abraham, and in each generation following, God chooses someone to carry it forward. In the generation after Abraham, it was Isaac, not Ishmael. And now, in the next generation, Jacob is picked for this great plan and blessing.

During her pregnancy, the mother Rebekah is disturbed by the violent activity in her womb as "the babies jostled each other" (Gen. 25:22). The word *jostled* is a strong word in the Hebrew language. It implies the twins were struggling with each other, fighting each other, smashing themselves into each other—the kind of violence that would cause damage to each other, maybe even a miscarriage of one or both. She asks God for an explanation. And the Lord replies:

> *Two nations are in your womb,*
> > *and two peoples from within you will be separated;*
> *one people will be stronger than the other,*
> > *and the older will serve the younger."* (Gen. 25:23)

With these words, God repeats to the next generation his promise of a multitude of descendants. And before the boys are born, he chooses the twin he plans to bless and use as part of his purpose. Look closely at the four lines of verse 23:

The first line—"Two nations are in your womb." Twins in there! And these twins will become the ancestors of nations. Both of them will have millions of descendants; both will become a nation of people—Arabs and Jews.

The second line—These two nations will not be able to live together. The "two peoples within you will be separated." They will act so violently against each other that they will have to live apart. Constant turmoil in the Middle East, constant warfare between Arabs and Jews.

The third line—One of the nations, however, will dominate. "One people will be stronger than the other." One of these boys, and the nation or people descended from him, will be chosen to continue God's plan; one of them will become God's means of blessing the world. Which one?

Well, the older one, of course—right? Isn't that the expectation in the culture—the expectation that the oldest will carry on the leadership? The right of the firstborn.

But no, the last line—the older one will not dominate. Instead, "the older will serve the younger." Against all expectation, God is picking the younger. God will work through the younger. God will bless the world through the younger.

Before they are born, God already knows his plans. Before they are born, God already has decided which one will carry forward his purpose: the younger.

When the time came for Rebekah to give birth, "the first to come out was red, and his whole body was like a hairy garment; so they named him Esau. [*Esau* sounds a lot like the Hebrew word for "hairy."] After this, his brother came out, with his hand grasping Esau's heel; so he was named Jacob [*Jacob* means "heel-grabber"]."

Jacob is the younger! And as he comes into the world, God already has a specific purpose for his life.

But that's not just true of Jacob. It's also true of you—God brought you into the world for a specific purpose, and he has a plan to bless you beyond imagination. You were not just a twinkle in your parents' eyes. Over and over the Scriptures tell us that God has a plan for your life, and his intention is to bless you beyond any anything you expect.

> *For you created my inmost being;*
> *you knit me together in my mother's womb.*
> *My frame was not hidden from you*
> *when I was made in the secret place,*
> *when I was woven together in the depths of the earth.*
> *Your eyes saw my unformed body;*
> *all the days ordained for me were written in your book*
> *before one of them came to be. (Ps. 139:13, 15–16)*

Before you were born, God knew his plans for you, and he's constantly thinking of the blessing he has prepared for you:

> *The word of the LORD came to me, saying,*
> *"Before I formed you in the womb I knew you,*
>   *before you were born I set you apart;*
>   *I appointed you as a prophet to the nations." (Jer. 1:4–5)*

Before you were born, God knew how he was going to use you. Paul realized that even before he became a believer, God had a plan for his life, to bless him and use him:

> *For you have heard of my previous way of life in Judaism, how intensely I persecuted the church of God and tried to destroy it. I was advancing in Judaism beyond many of my own age among my people and was extremely zealous for the traditions of my fathers. But when God, who set me apart from my mother's womb and called me by his grace, was pleased to reveal his Son in me so that I might preach him among the Gentiles . . . (Gal. 1:13–16)*

And what was true of him, Paul writes, is true of all Christians:

> *For we are God's handiwork, created in Christ Jesus to do good works, which God prepared in advance for us to do. (Eph. 2:10)*

God has a reason for your existence. He brought you into this world to bless you and use you. You were a "planned pregnancy." God intended your birth, and he also has a plan for your life.

Now, the question is: How do you fulfill it? What response will enable you to enjoy God's blessing and fulfill his purpose? You may sense that God's purpose and blessing is somehow related to your job or your career. Or to your marriage, your children, your church, or community service. You may have some sense of what God's plan is. How do you get it? What response does God ask from you?

The answer of our passage is: Don't grab for it. Don't do anything to force it. Don't scheme or plot or maneuver to make it happen. Don't say, "God has planned this for me, so I'm going to force it to happen." Don't grab.

Jacob will have to fight that tendency all his life—the tendency to grab, to force, to maneuver, to manipulate. He comes into the world with the promise that God will bless him beyond anything he can imagine, but from the moment of his birth he can't trust God to give it to him, and so he grabs and manipulates and schemes to get it.

Even as he's born, as he comes out of the womb, he is grabbing. As the boys are born, Jacob has his hand on his brother's heel, as though he knows it's usually the firstborn in the culture who gets the blessing, and he wants to pull his brother by the heel back into the womb: "No, me first." And his parents name him Jacob—heel-grabber. Heel-grabber—someone trying to pull others back so that he can be first, someone who wants to get ahead, someone on the make, someone around whom you have to watch your back—a manipulator, a schemer, a plotter.

All through his life Jacob will continue that pattern—not trusting God to give him what he promised, but maneuvering, dealing, conniving, taking advantage of others' weaknesses to get what he wants, to get what he believes God has for him. He will lie and plot and scheme to get the blessing he believes God intends for him.

As we follow his life, we'll see that he wants God's blessing so badly, he'll compromise his integrity, and in the process fill himself with fear and misery. He'll rupture his relationships—his family and relatives will become so furious with him that they'll want to destroy him. He'll breed suspicion and hatred and retaliation—others will treat him as he treated them, with the same manipulation, the same deception. He'll feel attacked on all sides.

And there will be times in his grabbing when it will look like he has blown the plan to smithereens. But in spite of all this, God will keep his promise. The blessing God said he would give—it will come.

Along the way, God will teach him, "Don't grab. Trust me to give." God will teach him, gently, patiently, over and over again, "Don't force it. I've promised. It will come."

God will say to him and to us, "I'll keep my promise. I have a plan for your life, and there is a time in my plan when the blessing will come. Trust me."

The reason we might be tempted to grab is because God's timing may not be as soon as we want it. We want it *now*. And so we may be tempted to scheme and maneuver, to force it to come.

We may want that marriage and family that God has for us so badly that when it doesn't look like it's happening, and we're going with someone, we may be tempted to compromise our purity, or lie about our past, in order to hang on to this person, to keep him or her attached to us. We think, "This is what I need to do to get what God has for me." Instead of trusting God to bring it in his time, we compromise or lie. But the result is sorrow and regret.

We may want that job or promotion, with the higher income and greater satisfaction, so badly that if it doesn't look like it's happening, we may be tempted to lie on a resume, or apple-polish, or undermine others in order to force what God has for us. But the end result is disgust and shame.

We may want God's future for our children so badly that when they get in a jam and it looks like their future is in jeopardy, we may bail them out with our money or our influence. To give them the blessing we believe God has for them, we might be tempted to lie about our address to get them into a better school. Or somewhere along the line we start doing more for them, or giving them more than we should, and the overindulgence weakens their character instead of making them strong for God's purposes.

We want God's blessing so badly we may be tempted to grab for it, to force it, to get it now. But instead all we get is sorrow and conflict. If we sin to make God's purpose happen, if we compromise ourselves to get it, we only create turmoil and regret. And the blessing will not come sooner than God intends.

God tells us over and over again that he knows the timing. It may not be as soon as we think, or as soon as we want. But he will bring it.

Jacob should have known that. Jacob should have seen it in the history of his family. His father before him, and his grandfather before that—both of them had had to wait for God's timing before the blessing came.

God gave the original promise to his grandfather when he was seventy-five years old: "I'll give you millions of descendants." But at that time Abraham had no children, and his wife Sarah was unable to conceive. You can't have millions of descendants unless you start with at least one child. After ten years of waiting for the promise, and not seeing it coming, Abraham took matters into his own hands. His wife had a maid named Hagar, and according to the customs of the day, a maid was considered the personal property of the wife. And any child born from her was considered as an adopted son or daughter. And so Abraham, at age eighty-five, fathers a child by Hagar. That child was Ishmael. But that was not God's plan. And grabbing for it only produced conflict and regret.

Abraham continued to wait for God's timing—another five years, ten years, fifteen years. And when he was one hundred years old, God fulfilled his promise to Abraham, in a way no one expected. His wife Sarah—all her life unable to conceive, and now, at age ninety, way beyond anybody's ability to conceive—Sarah gets pregnant. What a laugh! And they named the child Isaac—which in Hebrew means "laughter." God knew his plan, and in his time he brought his blessing, in a way no one could expect.

Jacob should have known that from his grandfather Abraham. And he should have known it from his father Isaac also. Isaac married late in life—forty years old (Gen. 25:20). Isaac too had the promise—he would carry forward God's plan of millions of descendants who would bless the world. But he too doesn't have even one child—his wife Rebekah is barren for twenty years (25:21). Year after year, as time passes, for twenty years, Isaac prays, wondering when and how will God fulfill his promise and send the blessing. And then after twenty years, the twins are born.

Jacob should have known from his father and his grandfather that nothing limits God, and that there is a time in his plan when the blessing will come. Wait for it, Jacob. Don't grab it. God will give it.

And that, my friend, is God's word to you. Don't grab it. God will give it. Wait. And as you wait, pray. Pray as Isaac did, if necessary for twenty years—for that shows you're aware of God's promise, and you're waiting for his plan. Pray as Rebekah did, to find out what was going on in her womb—for that helps you to understand what God is doing in your life along the way.

Pray to a God who is not limited in any way, who can do beyond what you expect. To a God who says, "The younger shall be first. The barren will conceive. The aged will give birth." Pray to a God who is not limited by your education, or geography, or age, or finances, or family, or circumstances—a God who knows his plan and will make it happen.

Pray with a quiet confidence. There is a time in God's plan when the blessing will come.

Don't grab it. God will give it.

2

"GIMME SOME OF THAT RED STUFF"

Genesis 25:27–34

Linda Ellerbee is a well-known name in media circles. As a longtime correspondent for NBC news, she covered Congress, the White House, presidential campaigns, and national conventions. Mostly, however, she was known for her newspaper column, which was syndicated nationally.

Several years ago, she developed cancer as a result a lifetime of smoking. She had mastectomies and other treatments to combat the disease. Following her treatment, in one of her columns, she writes about smoking, about cancer, and about children.[*]

> The phone rings. The person on the other end says that Paul, an old friend, has lung cancer and will be operated on the next day. I am shocked. Sure, Paul was a heavy smoker, but Paul quit smoking *five years* ago. Now he gets lung cancer? Where's the fairness in that, I ask no one in particular, although I know the answer. Fairness has nothing to do with it. Paul is learning in the hardest way possible that not all the consequences of smoking disappear when one stops, at least not quickly. Paul quit smoking when he was 51, but Paul started smoking when he was 11. Forty years of cigarettes will not be ignored.
>
> As someone who smoked a long time and quit only two years ago, I pay close attention to Paul's story—and though I promised myself I would never become one of those nasty ex-smokers who tries to make

---

[*] *Austin American Statesman*, February 3, 1995.

everyone who smokes feel like the dirt of the earth, I find I have less and less tolerance for second-hand smoke.

We know how harmful smoking is—according to the Centers for Disease Control, tobacco addiction kills more than 418,000 Americans each year. That's more than alcohol, cocaine, crack, heroin, homicide, suicide, fires, car accidents, and AIDS *combined.* . . .

The good news is that only 26 percent of all Americans still smoke. The bad news is that according to the American Heart Association, 3,000 children begin smoking every day.

I think about that figure a lot, and I know in my heart that, while heavy advertising by tobacco-product makers to the youth market is partly responsible for this sorry statistic, as is the glamorizing of smoking one still sees on television and in movies, many of these children smoke, or will smoke, because they have a parent who does.

It is now two years and one month since I quit smoking. Quitting was incredibly hard and, yes, there are still times I would give almost anything for a cigarette, but I know I've done the right thing by quitting, and I feel good about it; however, no matter how fine I might feel about the choice I've made, nothing can make up for this: Both my grown children smoke.

Wonder where they learned that? "Nothing can make up for this: Both my grown children smoke."

Decisions she made twenty years ago when her children were small, decisions about smoking, decisions she can't now change—these decisions are affecting her children today.

Some decisions that we seemingly make for the moment have an impact on the future that can never be changed

You and I may not make decisions about smoking. But we make other decisions—decisions that seem like they're just for the moment, but which can have an impact on the future that can never be changed.

Maybe we make a decision about divorce—a decision that may bring an end to present conflict, but which might also risk the well-being or dysfunction of our children for decades, making them part of the statistics of those who carry the baggage and consequences into their adult lives of what their parents did years earlier.

Maybe we make a decision about how regularly we will bring our children to church. Sometimes the decision *not* to come to church on a given Sunday seems so minor. Families decide instead to go away for the weekend. Or parents decide to put their children in soccer leagues where the games conflict with Sunday services. Or they decide to let a child stay home from church because the child was out late last night, or because the child is grumpy and out of sorts, or simply because the child doesn't want to go to church today. "OK, OK, stay home." Seems like a minor decision.

But such decisions, seemingly for the moment, for a given Sunday, may have an impact on the future. The parents who make the decision—there's no question they have a passion for God. But the child, who has not yet developed that passion, is getting a different message—the message that many things can come ahead of God; God takes second place to soccer, or sleep-overs, or your grumpy moods. The parents, whose own commitment to God was nurtured and cemented through a childhood of never-miss attendance, are not passing on to their child the same habit and the same passion. And the child grows up with God on the periphery rather than at the center of life.

Some of the decisions we make for the moment can have an impact for the future that cannot be changed.

We're going to look at two brothers, actually fraternal twins—they don't look alike, but they were born only moments apart. Brothers who are both faced with a decision, the same decision.

As one of the brothers makes the decision, he has his eye on the future. He knows his decision, made now, will affect his children, and their children, and their children. And as he faces this decision, he thinks of the generations that will come from him, and everything about his decision is driven by his desire that God would be part of their lives, that God would bless them and use them.

The other brother faces the same decision. But he gives no thought to what impact his decision will have on future generations. What's important is *him*, his comfort, right now. He bases his decision on immediate convenience, something that will please him at the moment. He chooses a short-term personal gain, and he forfeits a long-term family blessing.

One brother protects God's blessing on his children for generations to come. The other brother forever surrenders his family's spiritual future.

The story of these two brothers will help us to choose well when we face some of our decisions—decisions we think are only for the moment, but which can determine the future for generations.

The two brothers are opposites. As they grow to young adulthood, their personalities differ in every way. As sometimes happens in families, each parent has a favorite—the father favors the older brother, the mother favors the younger.

The two brothers are Esau and Jacob. We're going to pick up the story shortly after their birth. We'll see the contrast, the difference, between the two brothers. This contrast will prepare us for the decision they face—a decision that will move their families in different directions forever.

First, we'll notice the contrast, the difference between the two brothers as they grow up. They are opposites. Their personalities differ in every way.

The boys grew up, and Esau became a skillful hunter, a man of the open country, while Jacob was content to stay at home among the tents. Isaac, who had a taste for wild game, loved Esau, but Rebekah loved Jacob. (Gen. 25:27–28)

The boys are opposites. Esau, the older brother, is a skillful hunter, a man who roams the open country. Jacob, the younger brother, is "content to stay at home among the tents." These two descriptions are designed to highlight the difference between the brothers. They point out the deep contrast in their characters. One man is undisciplined, impulsive. The other one is thoughtful, in control.

Esau, the older son, is the undisciplined one. He's restless, unsettled, impulsive. He has become a hunter, which is a way of saying that he has chosen a restless, erratic, inconsistent life. Hunting doesn't take the discipline of a daily routine; you only get up and go out when you think you need something.

But the family never really needs Esau to go out and hunt. They don't need the food he brings in. Their economics, their survival, doesn't require it. The family has a huge ranching operation. They have thousands of sheep, thousands of cattle—vast herds of domestic animals to butcher for the food they need.

Further, it's not as though the wild game is plentiful or overpopulating, and Esau's hunting is necessary to thin out the herds. On the contrary, the game he hunts is scarce, hard to find. In fact, it's only because Esau has developed a bit of skill that he ever has any success at all. Most of the time, as we'll see in a moment, when he comes back from one of his hunts—even though he's been gone for days at a stretch—he's empty-handed.

There's nothing about Esau's hunting that is necessary or essential to the family. It's just difficult to keep him focused and productive at home. He'd rather roam the open country. He's unsettled, impulsive, undisciplined.

Jacob, by contrast, is a *contented* man. In the Hebrew language that means a thoughtful man, a man who reflects on things, an even-tempered man who thinks things through, perhaps even a calculating man—a shrewd, discerning man.

And he's also described as one who chooses to "stay at home among the tents." That means he's a settled man, useful to the family business. Instead of disappearing for days at a time in the open country, he stays among the encampment of tents, and helps with the ranching, the shepherding, the breeding, the watering, the pasturing. We would say he's learning the family business—moving from sales to accounting to research and development to legal to human resources. He's "among the tents"—a settled, useful man. And he is a patient man, for shepherding takes great patience and watching and waiting.

Esau is undisciplined, impulsive. Jacob is thoughtful and can bide his time.

One day these two brothers each make a decision, a decision that changes their lives and the lives of their children forever. On this day, during a conversation between them, they make a trade, a swap. The older brother hands over the birthright; the younger brother hands over a bowl of stew. The older brother hands over his spiritual future; the younger brother hands over a pot of food. And from that moment on, the destinies of their children move in different directions forever.

Look at this decision—this trade, this swap:

Once when Jacob was cooking some stew, Esau came in from the open country, famished. He said to Jacob, "Quick, let me have some of that red stew! I'm famished!" (That is why he was also called Edom [which means "red"]).

Jacob replied, "First sell me your birthright."

"Look, I am about to die," Esau said. "What good is the birthright to me?"

But Jacob said, "Swear to me first." So he swore an oath to him, selling his birthright to Jacob.

Then Jacob gave Esau some bread and some lentil stew. He ate and drank, and then got up and left.

So Esau despised his birthright. (Gen. 25:29–34)

Esau sells his birthright. What is this birthright?

In their culture, the *birthright* was the right of the "first-birth" to be the leader of the clan, the right of the firstborn to be the head of the extended family—brothers, sisters, nieces, nephews, second and third generation grandchildren. It was a position of leadership and privilege that was passed down to the firstborn of each generation, continuing for generation after generation. In their culture, the birthright was an inherited position of authority and respect. It meant prestige and honor for the future.

This is what the birthright meant in their culture—authority, prestige, leadership for the future. But for these two brothers, the birthright meant even more than that. For these two brothers, the birthright not only meant honor and leadership in the family, it also meant the eternal blessing of God. In their family, God had attached his blessing to the birthright. Whoever had the birthright also had the blessing.

In their culture, the birthright and the blessing are so closely associated that they sound almost the same in the Hebrew language. The same letters are used; just a couple of them are reversed.

birthright—*bekora*
blessing—*beraka*

In their family, whoever had the *bekora* had the *beraka*. The blessing went with the birthright.

What was this blessing? The blessing was God's promise to work through that line of the family to bless the entire world, his promise to carry forward his purposes in the world through that side of the family. The blessing was God's promise that he would make that line the most prominent family on earth, and bring a Savior into the world through them. The blessing was the promise that they would be the greatest family in history, and the entire world would be indebted to them.

You can see this promise, this blessing, just a few chapters earlier, as God gives it for the very first time to Abraham, the grandfather of these two brothers. When God had called Abraham to leave the country he was living in and come to the new land where they were now, God had promised the blessing to Abraham—that Abraham would be the start of the greatest family in history, and that the entire world would be blessed through his family.

> *I will make you into a great nation,*
> *and I will bless you;*
> *I will make your name great,*
> *and you will be a blessing.*
> *I will bless those who bless you,*
> *and whoever curses you I will curse;*
> *and all peoples on earth*
> *will be blessed through you.* (Gen. 12:2–3)

Abraham passed the blessing on to his son Isaac. And now one of these boys will get it next—the birthright and the blessing, God's promise that he will work through one line of the family and his descendants to bless the entire world.

Under normal circumstances, all of this belongs to Esau. He's the older brother; he's the firstborn, the first birth. The birthright and the blessing that comes with it—under normal circumstances, are his.

But in one moment's decision, he changes the direction of his family forever. For a short-term gain, he forfeits the long-term blessing. For the convenience of a moment, he surrenders his family's spiritual future. He trades the birthright for a bowl of stew.

Look how it happens:

> Once when Jacob was cooking some stew, Esau came in from the open country, famished. He said to Jacob, "Quick, let me have some of that red stew! I'm famished!" (That is why he was also called Edom.) Jacob replied, "First sell me your birthright." (Gen. 25:29–31)

The way this is written suggests that Jacob has carefully planned for this moment. He's a thoughtful, calculating man, and he's figured out how to get what he wants, how to take advantage of his brother's impulsiveness and lack of discipline. He's shrewdly set things up so that he can catch Esau at a weak moment. The verses are written in such a way as to suggest this careful planning.

For example, verse 29 says that when Esau came in from hunting, he found Jacob cooking. The word for *cooking* in their language sounds a lot like the word for *hunting*.

hunting—*zayid*
cooking—*zid*

Esau had been out hunting—*zayid*—for game, but now Jacob is *zid*—hunting for Esau. Jacob knows that Esau's been gone all day, and there's a good chance he'll return empty-handed, as he usually does. And Jacob is hunting him, with his cooking, laying a trap for him as he comes back.

Jacob has positioned himself along the route he expects Esau to use coming back, maybe about an hour from camp. He settles his sheep into a pasture, and he starts cooking. He's brought along a pot of minestrone stew—red beans mixed with onions, spices, and marbled beef with the animal fat that gives a delicious taste. About the time he expects Esau to return, he gets the fire going, the pot simmering and bubbling, and the delicious smell wafts itself on the breeze. Kind of like when you're outside your house and you sniff and say, "Somebody's barbecuing tonight. Sure smells good!"

Esau, on his way back, catches the tantalizing whiff, and follows it to his brother's fire. Esau hasn't eaten all day. His stomach is growling. His blood sugar is low. He sees and smells the stew, thinks of what the hot food would taste like, how good it will feel in his mouth, how comfortable his full stomach will feel. He thinks of the pleasure of the moment. And he says, "Hey, Jacob, gimme some of that red stuff, that red stuff there. I'm starving."

That's what Jacob's waiting for, and he's ready. His answer is short and to the point: "I'll trade it to you for the birthright. Give me the birthright for it."

There's nothing commendable about what Jacob is doing. There's nothing admirable in his action. He's scheming and manipulating. He's taking advantage of his brother's weakness. But the reason he's doing it is because *he* wants the blessing that comes with the birthright. He wants God's activity in *his* family. He wants *his* children to be blessed by God. He wants God to use *them*. He wants God close to *his* family for generations to come. He doesn't want it to read, "Abraham, Isaac, and Esau." He wants it to read, "Abraham, Isaac, and Jacob." And so he says, "Sell me the birthright."

Esau's response is, "Sure. Why not? What good is the birthright? Who cares about it? You can have it. Give me stew."

> *"Look, I am about to die," Esau said. "What good is the birthright to me?"* (Gen. 25:32)

When Esau says, "I am about to die," he doesn't mean that he's within a few hours of keeling over from starvation. No. Many times, when he's been out hunting, he's gone hours, days, without food. And his family's home camp, where he can get all the food he wants, is at most just a few miles away. He could be sitting down to a hot meal in less than an hour. He's not making an exaggerated statement: "I'm dying; I have to have something to eat right away."

When he says, "I am about to die," what he means is, "As a hunter, I've chosen a lifestyle where I could die at any moment, and what good will the birthright do me then? When I'm miles away hunting, I could step in a hole and break a leg, and never make it back to camp. Or some animal might leap on me and maul me, and I'd bleed to death before anybody thinks to look for me. Anytime I go out may be my last time. What value to me is something as far off in the future as a birthright? I might not live to see it."

Even if he might somehow manage to die peacefully in old age, his attitude is, "What good is the birthright?" He doesn't see that there's any benefit that comes from having the birthright and blessing.

What is the blessing? To inherit a land and be the chosen family through whom God works to influence the world. How likely are those things to happen? Not very. As far as Esau is concerned, it's all pretty iffy.

His grandfather Abraham had the birthright and the blessing. How much of the land did he ever own? One cave hole in the side of a hill, to bury his wife, and where they later buried him (Gen. 23:17–20; 25:9–10). That's all.

His father Isaac inherited it next. The birthright and blessing were passed down to him. Has he gained any more of the promised land? No. The family doesn't own a single acre. They dig wells, but the citizens force them to move (Gen. 26:12–23). They're not inheriting the land and they're not influencing the world. And as far as Esau can see, these things are not going to happen in his lifetime.

Is God working in their clan? Is God committed to their family? Who's to say? Where's the evidence? Maybe he is and maybe he isn't. You can talk about God's promises and God's purposes, but to Esau it's pretty vague and remote. "When I'm gone, what do I care what happens, if anything? I won't be here to see it. What do I care about some intangible blessing? It's all there and then, maybe. This is here and now. What good is the birthright? You can have it. Give me some stew."

"Not so fast," Jacob says. "Swear to me that I can have it. Take an oath, something that can never be changed. Swear first."

> But Jacob said, "Swear to me first." So he swore an oath to him, selling his birthright to Jacob. Then Jacob gave Esau some bread and some lentil stew. He ate and drank, and then got up and left. So Esau despised his birthright. (Gen. 25:33–34)

Esau swears an oath. "I swear that you can have the birthright. It has little value to me." He gives up the long-term blessing for the short-term gain. He surrenders his family's future for a momentary pleasure, an immediate convenience. He trades the birthright for stew. He eats, he drinks, he gets up and he leaves—with no thought for what his decision means for the future.

The account ends, "So Esau despised his birthright." He attached no weight or importance to it at all. He gave no thought to what impact his decision would have on his family's future. He did not concern himself with God's plans, with God's presence and activity in his family. For a momentary convenience, he forfeited his family's spiritual future.

The New Testament looks back on this man and says, "Don't be like him." The New Testament looks back on Esau's decision, on the choice he made, and says, "Don't do as this man did." The author of Hebrews warns us that a decision, seemingly for the moment, can have an impact on the future that can never be changed.

> *See that no one . . . is godless like Esau, who for a single meal sold his inheritance rights as the oldest son. Afterward, as you know, when he wanted to inherit this blessing, he was rejected. Even though he sought the blessing with tears, he could not change what he had done.* (Heb.12:16–17)

There will come a time in the next couple of chapters in Genesis where we will see Esau regret his action. He will bitterly regret the decision. He will want to turn back the clock, but will be unable to do so. He will weep, the tears will flow, but it will be beyond change. The blessing and the birthright are gone forever. Do not be like this godless man.

My friend, when a moment of decision comes to you, look into the future. Think about the next generation. The choices you make now can determine your children's spiritual lives for years to come.

Choose that attendance at church on Sunday is a priority for your family.

Choose that whatever else your family spends money on, there will always be money for mission trips, youth camps, and church activities, so that your children will fall in love with God.

Choose that the amount of your family's giving to the Lord in any given year will always be greater than what you spend on annual passes or vacations or eating out, so that the children will see that God is most important.

Choose to love your spouse through all the difficulties and hard stretches. Choose to love your spouse and stay together no matter what, so that the kids will grow into their adult years secure and stable.

Choose how many hours a week you will work and who will be home after school, so that you are there to build godly values into the children.

Choose that certain cable stations will not be on your TV and certain rated videos will not be brought into your home.

Make the decisions now that can affect the future and perhaps even generations to come.

Choose to love your God.

Choose to keep his blessing on your kids.

3

FORSAKING FAMILY FLAWS

Genesis 26:1–11

We all tell ourselves that when we grow up, we're not going to be like our parents. We're not going to say the things they said or act the way they did.

When we were kids, and we asked our parents why we couldn't do something, they said, "Because." "Why because?" "Because I said so, that's why." And we vowed we'd never say that to our kids . . . but we do.

When our parents gave us the third degree—"Where are you going, who are you going with, how late will you be?"—we made up our minds that when *we* had kids we'd be more trusting of them. And so we say to *our* kids, "Where are you going, who are you going with, how late will you be? . . . That's too late!" How quickly we become "a chip off the old block" and repeat the behaviors of our parents.

And the last thing we want is for somebody to point this out to us—that we're acting like our parent. The surest way I know to set myself up for a bad few days is to say to my wife, Nell, "You're acting just like your mother." Not a smart thing to say. And *(I say indignantly)* I don't know why she sees traits of my father in me!

There's humor in this. But there's also some sadness, because often the most damaging patterns of our lives are shaped by the homes we grew up in. This sad truth shows up most severely in child abuse. Study after study reveals that most parents who abuse their children were themselves abused by their parents.

For most of us, the problem is not this severe. But it's still there, because in times of stress or threat, we too often find ourselves repeating the patterns of our parents.

To avoid hassles, we retreat into a newspaper or TV or a separate room of the house. That's what our dad did.

To end an argument, we make a cutting remark and slam a door behind us so that we don't have to hear any more. That's what our mom did.

We may struggle to manage our money or to avoid overspending. We may lie to get out of a tight situation. We may erupt in rage as a means of controlling the family and getting our way. That's what our parents did.

At the moment, these seem like the thing to do. At the time of stress or threat, they seem like the answer—the solution to our problem. They work!

But later, we know we were wrong to act that way. We see our children being damaged, our marriages being strained, our relationships with relatives, friends, and co-workers being torn, and we say, "God, help me. Help me break from the patterns of the past. Help me not to repeat the family flaws I've grown up with."

The good news is that God is ready to do that. We don't need the behaviors of the past to protect ourselves, to escape some threat, or to solve some problem. We don't need to repeat the damaging patterns of the past to have some good come to our life. God's love for us is so great, his goodness so certain, that we can trust him without fear. We can forsake the family flaw, because God's goodness will come to us without our behaving that way.

That's what God is trying to say that to Jacob—that he doesn't need to repeat his family's destructive patterns. He can forsake the family flaw because God's goodness will come to him without it.

A very damaging flaw has come down through Jacob's family. He saw the flaw very obviously in his grandfather Abraham. Now he sees the same flaw repeated in his father Isaac. And he's beginning to see the same tendency in himself.

And God's gentle urging to him, and to us, is, "You don't need to repeat the family flaw, you have my promise—my goodness comes to you without it."

We pick up the story as Jacob watches his father Isaac repeat the same wrong behavior of his grandfather Abraham, with the same damaging consequences. He sees his father, under stress, react to a threatening situation exactly like his grandfather did.[*]

The threat his father is facing is the threat of a famine—no water, no food, the collapse of the family's ranching business, and ultimately the starvation of the clan. His father makes a decision to relocate the family and the business closer to the seacoast. But this relocation takes them into the potentially hostile territory of the Philistines:

> Now there was a famine in the land—besides the previous famine in
> Abraham's time—and Isaac went to Abimelek king of the Philistines in
> Gerar. (Gen. 26:1)

A famine is threatening the family. It's probably been about two years since any rain has fallen in the area where Isaac has his flocks and herds. Two years with no water. Everything growing in the ground is drying up and turning black. The animals are shriveling and dying. The wells are empty— you drop a bucket down, but there's no water to bring up. So you lower children into the wells, with rags, to sop up whatever moisture there is, so that when they come up they can squeeze it into the mouths of sheep.

No water, no food—a famine. And unless something's done soon, Isaac's entire family and all his livestock will dehydrate and bloat and die. This is the stress, the threat Jacob's father is facing.

Isaac makes the decision to relocate his family and his flocks toward the Mediterranean coast, where the rains are more likely. But this decision means they'll be moving into a territory held by a pagan Philistine ruler whose behavior is unpredictable. This means the threat or danger to Isaac and his family won't necessarily go away, it'll just take a different form— hostility, harassment of the family.

But Jacob's father Isaac has little choice. It's either relocate or die. So he approaches the Philistine city of Gerar, and receives permission from the

---

[*] Since chapters 25–36 are the account, or history of Jacob, the insertion of two incidents concerning Isaac (26:1–11 and 26:12–33) are to be understood in terms of their impact on Jacob—i.e., what Jacob is to learn from them.

ruler of the city, Abimelek, to pasture his flocks on the outskirts while his family moves temporarily into the city.

As Jacob sees this threat of a famine develop, and watches his father react to it, he's aware that his grandfather had faced a similar situation. His family has been through this before—there had been the earlier famine of Abraham's time. We'll return to this in a moment.

Living in Gerar, Isaac becomes increasingly worried about the risks and unknowns of living in a pagan city—the potential hostility and harassment. He starts thinking about moving the family to Egypt instead. There's always food in Egypt. The Nile valley floods every year, creating rich pastures and farmlands. Maybe that would be a safer place for the family.

As Isaac ponders a move to Egypt, God comes to him and says, "Isaac, stay where you are. Don't go to Egypt. Stay in this land." God repeats the promise he will make again and again to this family—a promise of love, a promise of goodness, a promise of blessing. He says to Jacob's father, "I've brought you to this place. I'll be with you. And I'll keep my promises to you—promises of lands, promises of a family, and promises of a spiritual destiny."

God has already made these commitments to Jacob's grandfather Abraham (Gen. 12:1–3; 15:1–6; 17:1–8). Now, as God makes them again to his father Isaac, it's for the benefit of Jacob's ears, and ours—we can forsake the family flaw, because God's goodness will come to us without our engaging in that behavior.

God begins by saying to Isaac, "I've brought you to this place, to this land. Stay here."

> *The Lord appeared to Isaac and said, "Do not go down to Egypt; live in the land where I tell you to live. Stay in this land for a while . . ."* (Gen. 26:2–3a)

These words echo what God had earlier said to Jacob's grandfather Abraham—"Abraham, go to the land where I will tell you to live" (Gen. 12:1, paraphrase). Now God is saying to this family again, "This is the place I've brought you to, and where I want you to live. Stay here."

Then God continues, "Isaac, I will be with you in this place, in this situation. In all of its stresses and tensions, in all of its risks and unknowns, in all of its fears, its unpredictability, I will not abandon you:

Stay in this land for a while, and I will be with you and will bless you.
(Gen. 26:3a)

God will also speak these words to Jacob again and again. As we follow his life, we'll hear God repeating over and over, "Jacob, trust me. I'll be with you. My love for you is so great, my goodness to you is so certain, you can trust me without fear."

And finally God says to Jacob's father, "I'll keep my promises to you, promises of lands, promises of a family, and promises of a spiritual destiny. I've made a covenant; I've sworn an oath; I've given my word. And I'll keep my promises to you.

"First, I'll keep my promises regarding the lands:

Stay in this land for a while, and I will be with you and will bless you.
For to you and your descendants I will give all these lands and will con-
firm the oath I swore to your father Abraham. (Gen. 26:3)

"Second, I'll keep my promises regarding your family:

I will make your descendants as numerous as the stars in the sky and
will give them all these lands. (Gen. 26:4a)

"And finally, I'll keep my promises regarding your spiritual destiny in the future:

And through your offspring all nations on earth will be blessed.
(Gen. 26:4b)

In these words, Jacob hears again the family blessing that began with his grandfather Abraham, the blessing that is now being repeated to his father Isaac, and will also be God's sworn commitment to him—"I've led you in the past. I'll be with you in all situations. And I'll keep my promises to you. Therefore, Jacob, since this is so, forsake the family flaw. You don't need to repeat the family patterns of the past to protect yourself, to solve a problem, or to escape a threat. You don't need to repeat the destructive behavior of your father and grandfather to gain the good you want. I'll *give* it to you out of my love. You can forsake the family flaw because my goodness will come to you without it."

What is this family flaw that God wants him to forsake? What is the damaging behavior that has been repeated in his family from one generation to the next? What is it that Jacob's father does, just like his grandfather did? What is God trying to woo Jacob away from?

It's the flaw of deception—the pattern of lying, deceiving. Jacob's father reacts to the threatening famine situation the same way his grandfather did—with the same lie, the same deception, and the same damage to the family.

This flaw of lying and deceiving first showed itself in his grandfather Abraham. During the earlier famine in Abraham's time mentioned in verse 1, how does Abraham react to the threat at that time? With deception. He lies to protect himself, to solve his problem, to escape the threat.

When the famine hits, Abraham decides to relocate to Egypt, to the rich pastures and grazing areas around the Nile. But as Abraham approaches the border to Egypt, he's afraid. He's leaving the threat of the famine, but he's facing a new threat in Egypt: he's going into a pagan land, where Pharaoh's behavior is unpredictable.

Before he crosses the border, Abraham looks at his wife, Sarah, sees how beautiful she is, and realizes that when word reaches Pharaoh about the fair-skinned beauty who's just crossed his border, Pharaoh will want her to join his harem. If Sarah says to Pharaoh, "Mr. Pharaoh, I'm really flattered by your offer, but I already have a husband, Abraham here. I can't marry you, "Pharaoh will simply nod to one of his officers who will draw a sword and lop off Abraham's head. "Problem solved. Now you're free to marry me." All this goes through Abraham's mind. And so he attempts to protect himself with a lie. He resorts to deception to solve his problem, to escape the threat. He says to Sarah, "Tell everybody in Egypt that you're my sister, not my wife."

Now there was a famine in the land, and Abram went down to Egypt to live there for a while because the famine was severe. As he was about to enter Egypt, he said to his wife Sarai, "I know what a beautiful woman you are. When the Egyptians see you, they will say, 'This is his wife.' Then they will kill me but will let you live. Say you are my sister, so that I will be treated well for your sake and my life will be spared because of you."

When Abram came to Egypt, the Egyptians saw that Sarai was a very beautiful woman. And when Pharaoh's officials saw her, they praised her to Pharaoh, and she was taken into his palace. He treated Abram well for her sake, and Abram acquired sheep and cattle, male and female donkeys, male and female servants, and camels.

But the Lord inflicted serious diseases on Pharaoh and his household because of Abram's wife Sarai. So Pharaoh summoned Abram. "What have you done to me?" he said. "Why didn't you tell me she was your wife? Why did you say, 'She is my sister,' so that I took her to be my wife? Now then, here is your wife. Take her and go!" Then Pharaoh gave orders about Abram to his men, and they sent him on his way, with his wife and everything he had. (Gen. 12:10–20)

Facing the threat, Abraham lies.

Was this an isolated instance in Abraham's life? No. It happened again. It became a behavioral pattern—a flaw that would come down through the family.

Some years after this incident in Egypt, Abraham finds himself in another threatening situation, and he repeats the same lie. This time it happens in the very city of Gerar, where Isaac and the family are now living. Again, living in a pagan city, with an unpredictable ruler, Abraham once more feared for his life. And so he told the same lie: "Sarah is my sister." For a second time he compromised his wife, until God stepped in to clean up the mess.

Now Abraham moved on from there into the region of the Negev and lived between Kadesh and Shur. For a while he stayed in Gerar, and *there Abraham said of his wife Sarah, "She is my sister." Then Abi-melek* king of Gerar sent for Sarah and took her.* (Gen. 20:1–2)

Abimelek, the Philistine ruler, takes Sarah into his harem. Again God steps in.

> *But God came to Abimelek in a dream one night and said to him, "You are as good as dead because of the woman you have taken; she is a married woman."*
>
> *Now Abimelek had not gone near her, so he said, "Lord, will you destroy an innocent nation? Did he not say to me, 'She is my sister,' and didn't she also say, 'He is my brother'? I have done this with a clear conscience and clean hands."*
>
> *Then God said to him in the dream, "Yes, I know you did this with a clear conscience, and so I have kept you from sinning against me. That is why I did not let you touch her. Now return the man's wife, for he is a prophet, and he will pray for you and you will live. But if you do not return her, you may be sure that you and all who belong to you will die."* (Gen. 20:3–7)

The Philistine ruler quickly returns Sarah to Abraham, and says, "How could you have put me and my city in such a terrible danger?"

> *Early the next morning Abimelek summoned all his officials, and when he told them all that had happened, they were very much afraid. Then Abimelek called Abraham in and said, "What have you done to us? How have I wronged you that you have brought such great guilt upon me and my kingdom? You have done things to me that should never be done." And Abimelek asked Abraham, "What was your reason for doing this?"*
>
> *Abraham replied, "I said to myself, 'There is surely no fear of God in this place, and they will kill me because of my wife.' Besides, she really is my sister, the daughter of my father though not of my mother; and she became my wife. And when God had me wander from my father's*

---

* *Abimelek* is simply the title of the Philistine ruler. Just like *pharaoh* is the title for the Egyptian ruler. We also have titles today for our rulers: *president* or *prime minister*.

*household, I said to her, 'This is how you can show your love to me:
Everywhere we go, say of me, "He is my brother."'"* (Gen. 20:8–13)

A pattern of lying, deceiving—a behavioral flaw. Now Jacob is watching his father Isaac repeat the same behavior, in the same city, for the same reason. Now, a generation later, in the same city of Gerar, Jacob sees his father also distrust God's promise to be with the family and protect them, as Isaac resorts to the same deception, the same lie. And the family flaw shows itself again.

> *So Isaac stayed in Gerar.*
> *When the men of that place asked him about his wife, he said, "She is my sister," because he was afraid to say, "She is my wife." He thought, "The men of this place might kill me on account of Rebekah, because she is beautiful."*
> *When Isaac had been there a long time, Abimelek king of the Philistines looked down from a window and saw Isaac caressing his wife Rebekah.* (Gen. 26:6–8)

The king's palace is probably the highest building in the city. From a window high up the king can see into the deserted streets or into windows of other homes if people don't pull their curtains. One day he sees Isaac caressing or fondling Rebekah. "His sister, my eye. She's not his sister, she's his wife." And immediately he's afraid that some of his men might have acted inappropriately toward her, assuming she was single. He remembers what his father said would happen if any of them mistreated or dishonored the women of this family in any way. And he can't believe that the son of Abraham would do this to them again.

> *So Abimelek summoned Isaac and said, "She is really your wife! Why did you say, 'She is my sister'?" Isaac answered him, "Because I thought I might lose my life on account of her." Then Abimelek said, "What is this you have done to us? One of the men might well have slept with your wife, and you would have brought guilt upon us." So Abimelek gave orders to all the people: "Anyone who harms this man or his wife shall surely be put to death."* (Gen. 26:9–11)

A pattern of lying, deceiving. A family flaw that repeats itself from one generation to the next, from Abraham to Isaac. And the point here is to say to the next generation—to Jacob, who all his life will struggle with the same tendency to lie, to deceive—the point here of watching his father repeat the same fear and distrust of God, is to say to him, "Jacob, *you* don't need to act this way. I'll be with you. I'll keep my promises to you. You can forsake the family flaw. My goodness will come to you without it. My love for you is so great, my goodness to you is so certain, you can trust me without fear."

Can you hear God's gentle voice saying the same thing to you today? "My love for you is so great, my goodness to you is so certain, you can trust me without fear. You don't need the behaviors of the past to protect yourself, to escape a threat, to solve a problem. You don't need to repeat damaging patterns to gain some good in life. I will be good to you because I love you."

Forsake the family flaw. God's goodness will come to you without it.

4

IT IS "WELLS" WITH MY SOUL

Genesis 26:12–33

Some years ago I was pastoring a church in Austin, Texas. A number of lakes thread through the city of Austin. The church was located on the west side of one of the lakes, and so the name of the church was Westlake Bible Church.

A couple of blocks down the street from us, there was another church. This particular church was part of a hard-core fundamentalist denomination. It was a small church and getting smaller, because basically it was an unpleasant church—it was full of argumentative, bitter people. When visitors went once, they never went back.

The attendance at this church dwindled so much that one day a For Sale sign was posted in front of the church. We heard that if they could get a buyer, they were going to disband the church.

After a few months, the For Sale sign was taken down, and a new sign went up: Westbank Bible Church.

The new name was almost identical to ours, and it confused a lot of people. Some of our folk who drove by that church thought it was our name that was now on the site. They knew we were needing more space for classrooms, and assumed we had bought a suitable building to use just a couple of blocks away.

But we hadn't bought it, and we wondered who had. It turned out no one had bought it. There were no takers on the sale, so the church just decided to change its name and see if a new name might help their situation some. And so they picked a name almost identical to ours—just two letters different.

Our staff and elders began to wonder why they had chosen a name so similar to ours. We wanted to be charitable and give them the benefit of the doubt. But we wondered: Were they hoping that people who might be driving to visit us would wind up there instead? We had a good name in the community, and we were attracting people. Was this church trying to create some confusion, hoping to benefit from it?

Since the names were so similar, difficulties quickly followed. Mail started going to the wrong address. Delivery vans were showing up at the wrong location. We worried that if we ever had to call for an emergency vehicle, it might go to the wrong church.

So our associate pastor called the pastor of the other church and suggested that the similarity of our names was causing difficulties. And since we'd had our name for over twenty years, and they'd only had their new name for a few weeks, he asked if they would be willing to change it to something else.

The pastor of the church said he didn't see any problem; the names didn't seem that similar to him; he couldn't understand why there would be any confusion, and he didn't see any reason to consider a change.

Since we got nowhere with the pastor, our leadership began to wonder whether there was some other course of action we could take—maybe send a letter of appeal to the entire congregation? If that didn't work, then what?

This situation is a small example of something you might face in a far more serious way—where people see your good fortune, and try to seize it for themselves. They see God's favor on you, are envious of it, and try to grab it. They resent your success, and wrongfully try to gain it for themselves.

You may face it at work. Someone tries to hire away one of your company's key employees, hoping that will bring new clients to his company and enlarge his customer base, or maybe bring him some specialized technical skill or know-how he needs.

Maybe another company copies your new product line, or infringes on your logo, or intrudes into your franchise area.

Maybe you spend months putting together a deal. And then a competitor slanders you in such a way that the venture capitalists back out, or the investment partners put it on hold because now they're a bit uneasy, uncertain, maybe suspicious.

Once in a while the other person or company has enough influence or pull to freeze you out of new contracts, or make it difficult for you to lease space, or hinder you from arranging decent advertising.

Perhaps someone at work takes credit for your idea, or maneuvers and flatters to get a promotion that you deserved.

Maybe a supervisor denies you comp time or overtime pay.

One way or another, someone is envious of you, envious of God's goodness to you, and tries in some way to take it away from you.

In families, envious siblings might try to prevent you from getting a rightful share of the inheritance, or grab parental assets or furniture before a common decision can be made about distributing them, depriving you of what might be rightfully yours.

At school, someone who's envious of your success might steal a notebook from your backpack or check out all the required resources from the library so that you can't do your research. He might try to break up a friendship, or hit on your date. If he has influence, he may try to prevent others from sharing their class notes with you after you've missed a day.

I believe it was Mark Twain who once said, "There is always something about your success that displeases even your best friends."

There are times when people are envious of you, envious of God's goodness to you. And they want in some way to take it away from you; they want to hinder you from having it.

When this happens, our tendency is to fight back—to fight fire with fire, to call them down, to expose them publicly, to call attention to what they are doing so that others will side with us against them. We may even want to bring in the law, take them to court, sue them. Our tendency is to defend our rights, make an issue of it, protect what's rightfully ours.

But there's a reason you and I don't have to do that. We don't have to use any weapons or force against others who encroach on us. We don't have to defend ourselves or protect our rights.

The reason you and I don't need to hang on to the stuff is because God owns the supply. We don't need to clutch the money because God controls the mint.

This is something Jacob learns as he watches his father Isaac—you don't have to protect any particular blessing, because God will just keep the flow coming. No matter what envy or opposition or hostility you face, nothing can prevent God's goodness from coming to you. You can let go of the one because God will continually give you more.

Jacob learns this truth as he watches his father gain wealth beyond expectation. God, in his continuing goodness, gives the family unbelievable success in their business ventures:

> Isaac planted crops in that land and the same year reaped a hundred-fold, because the Lord blessed him. The man became rich, and his wealth continued to grow until he became very wealthy. He had so many flocks and herds and servants that the Philistines envied him. (Gen. 26:12–14)

"That land" is the seacoast land of the Philistines, where Isaac has moved because of a famine in the land of Canaan (Gen. 26:1). Planting crops is something new for the family, a new business venture. Up to now they've been ranchers and sheepherders.

But God gives them incredible success in their new business, wealth beyond expectation—an astounding yield per acre, an unbelievable return on their investment. They "reaped a hundredfold"—that's way beyond the average return. A hundredfold is the epitome of blessing. And the word *reaped* in the Hebrew language carries the idea of a surprised discovery—something way beyond normal. We're going to come across this word again and again in this passage—a surprised blessing beyond anything that could have been expected.

God's promise to this family is coming true—they are becoming great. The promise to Abraham years earlier:

> I will make you into a great [Heb. gadal] nation,
>> and I will bless you;
> I will make your name great [Heb. gadal] (Gen. 12:2)

is coming to pass:

The man became rich [great/gadal], and his wealth [greatness/ gadal] continued to grow until he became very wealthy [great/gadal]. (Gen. 26:13)

God's goodness is bringing success and wealth beyond imagination.

But God's favor leads to envy and opposition. The Philistines try to take the wealth away by destroying the family's wells—a hostile action intended to deprive the family of water needed for crops and animals, thus seriously threatening their income.

He had so many flocks and herds and servants that the Philistines en- vied him. So all the wells that his father's servants had dug in the time of his father Abraham, the Philistines stopped up, filling them with earth. (Gen. 26:14–15)

Now there is no water for their crops or animals. And then to top it off, the Philistine ruler tells them he wants them out of his area. His excuse is that his walled city can't handle the number of people Isaac has—his family and extended servants. There are too many of them—they're causing prob- lems in the cramped spaces.

Then Abimelek said to Isaac, "Move away from us; you have become too powerful for us." (Gen. 26:16)

Abimelek essentially freezes the family's assets and then tells them to leave.

Isaac doesn't have to take this. He doesn't have to let this happen. Isaac has the manpower to fight for his rights. He has a fighting force that's prob- ably superior to the Philistine's king—he could probably field an army large enough to win any battle with Abimelek. We read in an earlier chapter that his father Abraham had over three hundred trained servants that he armed and sent out for battle (Gen. 14:14). And the assumption is that Abraham's son Isaac has the same number of trained men at his disposal if he so wishes.

Isaac has the ability to fight for his assets, to beat down the opposition, and force his will on the situation. But instead, he chooses peace. Instead of fighting for his rights, which would cause havoc, bloodletting, and de- struction, Isaac chooses peace. Rather than forcing the issue, which would damage his reputation, destroy his relationships in the area, and leave behind wreckage, he chooses to let go of the one, believing that God will continually give him more.

He simply moves his entire family and operation fifteen miles away, and re-opens some old wells that his father Abraham had dug years ago.

> *So Isaac moved away from there and encamped in the Valley of Gerar, where he settled. Isaac reopened the wells that had been dug in the time of his father Abraham, which the Philistines had stopped up after Abraham died, and he gave them the same names his father had given them.* (Gen. 26:17–18)

Giving the same names to the wells is a way of re-establishing his title rights to them, and also shows his confidence that God will keep supplying his needs one way or another.

As the family continues to prosper in the new location, their success creates the need for even more water, more wells. So Isaac's servants begin digging forty or fifty feet into the ground, looking for a new source of water. And—here's our word again for a "surprised discovery"—they find a vast underground reservoir, beyond expectation.

> *Isaac's servants dug in the valley and discovered a well of fresh water there.* (Gen. 26:19)

But again there's opposition. As Yogi Berra said, "It's déjà vu all over again." The locals claim that the water belongs to them, and they seize the new well.

> *But the herders of Gerar quarreled with those of Isaac and said, "The water is ours!" So he named the well Esek* [dispute], *because they disputed with him.* (Gen. 26:20)

Isaac's servants then tap into the underground reservoir for another well, but the locals seize that one too.

> *Then they dug another well, but they quarreled over that one also; so he named it Sitnah* [opposition]. (Gen. 26:21)

As each well is disputed, Isaac realizes that there's going to be continual hostility to him in this area. So he's willing to move another ten miles, confident that no matter where he's forced to dig, or how often the wells are contested or stopped up, God will continue to provide.

He can let go of the one because God will continually give him more. And that's what happens.

> He moved on from there and dug another well, and no one quarreled over it. He named it Rehoboth [room], saying, "Now the Lord has given us room and we will flourish in the land." (Gen. 26:22)

Everything Isaac touches turns to water, because nothing can stop God's goodness to him. God then appears to him in a dream, and repeats his promises of blessing to the family.

> From there he went up to Beersheba. That night the Lord appeared to him and said, "I am the God of your father Abraham. Do not be afraid, for I am with you; I will bless you and will increase the number of your descendants for the sake of my servant Abraham." (Gen. 26:23–24)

Isaac's wealth keeps on increasing, so much so that his servants have to start digging again, exploring for even more water.

> Isaac built an altar there and called on the name of the Lord. There he pitched his tent, and there his servants dug a well. (Gen. 26:25)

By now Isaac has moved roughly a two-day distance from the Philistine king. And Abimelek has concluded that nothing he can do will stop the family's continued success. It's now obvious that God is going to bless this family no matter what. And Abimelek starts to worry that someday Isaac may seek revenge for how he's been treated. So the king travels two days with some of his cabinet officials to meet with Isaac, to negotiate grazing and water rights, and to seek a non-aggression treaty with him.

> Meanwhile, Abimelek had come to him from Gerar, with Ahuzzath his personal adviser and Phicol the commander of his forces. Isaac asked them, "Why have you come to me, since you were hostile to me and sent me away?"

They answered, "We saw clearly that the Lord was with you; so we said, 'There ought to be a sworn agreement between us'—between us and you. Let us make a treaty with you that you will do us no harm, just as we did not harm you but always treated you well and sent you away peacefully. And now you are blessed by the Lord." (Gen. 26:26–29)

They're putting a bit of a spin on it. They hadn't really sent him away in peace. But God's blessing is obvious. And Abimelek wants to be on good terms with Isaac.

By now Isaac is convinced of God's goodness. He doesn't need to fight over the past. He extends hospitality to them, makes a treaty with them, and sends them on their way in peace.

Isaac then made a feast for them, and they ate and drank. Early the next morning the men swore an oath to each other. Then Isaac sent them on their way, and they went away peacefully. (Gen. 26:30–31)

And God's goodness continues to pour in. For the third time we come across our word of a surprised discovery, a blessing beyond imagination.

That day Isaac's servants came and told him about the well they had dug. They said, "We've found [discovered a surprising quantity of] water!" He called it Shibah, and to this day the name of the town has been Beersheba. (Gen. 26:32–33)

My friend, you can let go of the one, for God will continually give you more. Here is God's blessing and benediction for you from Psalm 37:

Do not fret because of those who are evil
or be envious of those who do wrong;
for like the grass they will soon wither,
like green plants they will soon die away.

Trust in the Lord and do good;
dwell in the land and enjoy safe pasture.
Delight yourself in the Lord,
and he will give you the desires of your heart.

Be still before the Lord
    and wait patiently for him;
do not fret when men succeed in their ways,
    when they carry out their wicked schemes.
Refrain from anger and turn from wrath;
    do not fret—it leads only to evil.

Hope in the Lord
    and keep his way.
A future awaits for those who seek peace. (vv. 1–4, 7, 8, 34a, 37b)

You can let go of the one, for God will continually give you more.

5

MARRY CHRISTIANS, MERRY CHRISTIANS

Genesis 26:34–35; 27:46–28:9

I need four volunteers.

(Hold up two gunnysacks. Pick a couple of athletic teenagers as the first set of "volunteers." If possible, pick a couple of mismatched men for the second team—one tall, one short. Turn the two-man teams loose for a three-legged race through the auditorium, starting from opposite corners of the room, so that they have to cross each somewhere along the path. Hopefully, to the delight of their peers, the teenagers will decisively win the race, while the mismatched men stumble and fall. After the race, continue the message.)

When you're joined together, when you're bound together, you have to stride in sync to succeed. You have to get together to get to the goal.

If one of you has a longer leg, so that you step further than your partner, you'll soon stumble. In addition to stepping the same distance, you have to step with the same leg at the same time. And you have to keep the pace as you keep going—every stride has to be together.

And when you encounter others coming from the opposite direction, you have to decide together which side you're going to pass them on. You can't pull in opposite directions to get around them. If you do, you'll crash.

In previous centuries they probably didn't have three-legged races. But they were still clear on the same truth—you have to stride in sync to succeed. You have to get together to get to the goal.

Farmers knew this whenever they went plowing in one of their fields. They had to make sure that the two oxen yoked together were as evenly matched as possible. If one of the oxen was larger than the other, he would end up pulling most of the load, and would wear out more quickly. The best way to make the plowing succeed was to have them evenly matched in size and strength.

And then you had to train the oxen to walk stride for stride, to step at the same time, in the same pattern—right, left, front, back—keeping an even pressure on the yoke. You had to stride in sync to succeed.

It got even worse if you hooked up an ox on one side and a donkey on the other. It never worked. The ox would plod slowly. The donkey, one-third the size of the ox, would move with a quicker stride. Because of the uneven pulls, both animals ended up walking unnaturally. The plow would stop, start, stop, start hard for a few feet, stop, jerk, and both animals were soon worn out.

Also, the donkey would eat certain weeds along the way. And when he chewed the weeds, they gave off an odor or fume that was sickening to the ox. The ox would turn and walk sideways to get away from the nauseating fumes, and the plow would veer in a crooked direction. But since the ox couldn't get away because they were joined together, he would eventually become so affected by the noxious odor that he would almost pass out, and have to be practically dragged along.

You don't plow with an ox and donkey yoked together. This was so obvious to them, and such common knowledge, that it became kind of proverb of the day. In fact, these very words appear in the book of Deuteronomy:

Do not plow with an ox and a donkey yoked together. (Deut. 22:10)

When God says these words, however, he isn't giving farming advice. Everybody already knew that you don't join together two different animals. Instead, God is using that everyday picture to give a proverb about life and about marriage—about not joining a believer with an unbeliever in marriage. God is giving a principle for weddings—do not unite together as husband and wife a Christian and a non-Christian. Paul makes this clear in the New Testament. Writing to Christians living in the city of Corinth, he alludes to this Deuteronomy statement, explaining, "Here is what God is really saying:

> Do not be yoked together with unbelievers. For what do righteous- ness and wickedness have in common? Or what fellowship can light have with darkness? What harmony is there between Christ and Be- lial? Or what does a believer have in common with an unbeliever? (2 Cor. 6:14–15)

Do not be yoked with unbelievers. Do not marry a non-Christian.

You have to stride in sync to succeed, and you won't be able to do it. When you're joined together, when you're bound together, you have to work in harmony if you're going to get where you're going. And you can't do it if you don't share in your innermost heart the same eternal relationship to God. When one of you knows him and the other doesn't, at the very core of life you're out of sync. Everything will be out of step, and the result will be fatigue and falling down.

We see this so clearly in the Scriptures as we read about Jacob and Esau. God has a goal for Jacob's life. God has plans for him—he's going to work through him to bless the world. But in order for that to happen, Jacob must not marry an unbeliever.

Esau is just the opposite of Jacob. He has no concern for God's pur- poses. He doesn't care whether he is chosen for the purpose of blessing the world. The blessing, the promise—it's unimportant to him. And so, because of this disregard, he marries unbelievers—Canaanite women, Hittites.

The culture of the day allowed for more than one wife. The problem is not the number of Esau's wives. The problem is that the "gods" of these un- believers–their values, their interests—are in a different direction from the purposes God has for this family. And we read that Esau's marriage to these unbelievers brought grief to his parents:

> When Esau was forty years old, he married Judith daughter of Beeri the Hittite, and also Basemath daughter of Elon the Hittite. They were a source of grief to Isaac and Rebekah. (Gen. 26:34–35)

Rebekah resolves that the same thing must not happen with Jacob, their other son, the one in whom God had now centered his special purpose and destiny for the family. She knows God is going to carry forward his goals in Jacob—the blessing and the promise lie with him. But in order for Jacob to fulfill God's plan, he must not marry a Canaanite unbeliever as Esau did:

> Then Rebekah said to Isaac, "I'm disgusted with living because of these Hittite women. If Jacob takes a wife from among the women of this land, from Hittite women like these, my life will not be worth living." (Gen. 27:46)

Isaac agrees. Jacob must marry someone whose values and goals fit in with the special purpose God has. So he calls for his son and says, "You must go back to the area where are relatives are, and look for a wife from among them. And if you do, God will continue blessing you, and you will accomplish his special purpose for our family:

> So Isaac called for Jacob and blessed him. Then he commanded him: "Do not marry a Canaanite woman. Go at once to Paddan Aram, to the house of your mother's father Bethuel. Take a wife for yourself there, from among the daughters of Laban, your mother's brother. May God Almighty bless you and make you fruitful and increase your numbers until you become a community of peoples. May he give you and your descendants the blessing given to Abraham, so that you may take possession of the land where you now reside as a foreigner, the land God gave to Abraham." (Gen. 28:1–4)

This command—"Do not marry a Canaanite; do not marry an unbeliever"—was not simply a command for Jacob. It became a command for all his descendants who would follow—a command repeated again and again down through the generations. God has chosen this family-line to bless the world. But in order to do this, the descendants must not marry those whose gods are different, whose values and interests go in a different direction. God will say to his people again and again, "If you marry unbelievers, they will draw you away from me and from the goals I have for you."

When he brings his people out of Egypt, he tells them in the wilderness that he's going to take them into the land he had promised them. But he warns them that once they are in the land they must not marry the unbelievers there, for they would lead them away from him:

> Be careful not to make a treaty with those who live in the land; for when they prostitute themselves to their gods and sacrifice to them, they will invite you and you will eat their sacrifices. And when you choose some of their daughters as wives for your sons and those daughters prostitute themselves to their gods, they will lead your sons to do the same. (Exod. 34:15–16)

To marry an unbeliever is to marry someone who will draw you away from God and from the goals he has for your life.

This command has to be repeated to the next generation, because the wilderness generation that came out of Egypt never makes it into the land. They get up to the border, but then they draw back when they see the people they would have to fight to gain the land. "We're like grasshoppers compared to them," they say. And because of their lack of trust in God, they wander in the wilderness for forty years until they die off. Then God gets ready to take the next generation in. But before he does so, Moses repeats the command to them: "Do not marry the unbelievers in the land."

> When the Lord your God brings you into the land you are entering to possess . . . you must destroy them totally. Make no treaty with them, and show them no mercy. Do not intermarry with them. Do not give your daughters to their sons or take their daughters for your sons, for they will turn your children away from following me to serve other gods, and the Lord's anger will burn against you and will quickly destroy you. . . . For you are a people holy to the Lord your God. The Lord your God has chosen you out of all the peoples on the face of the earth to be his people, his treasured possession. (Deut. 7:1–6)

God has a special goal for your life. To marry an unbeliever is to be pulled away from that.

The next generation does enter the land under Joshua, conquering it and subduing the different groups living there. But before they settle in, Joshua has one last message to give them. And in his farewell address before he dies, he repeats this command to them: "In order for God to fulfill his purposes for you, you must not marry the unbelievers in the land."

> *The Lord has driven out before you great and powerful nations; to this day no one has been able to withstand you. . . . So be very careful to love the Lord your God.*
>
> *But if you turn away and ally yourselves with the survivors of these nations that remain among you and if you intermarry with them and associate with them, then you may be sure that the Lord your God will no longer drive out these nations before you. Instead, they will become snares and traps for you, whips on your backs and thorns in your eyes, until you perish from this good land, which the Lord your God has given you.* (Josh. 23:9–13)

Their strength will depend on walking close with God, but if they marry unbelievers, they'll find themselves drawn away from God's good plans for them.

Unfortunately, this is exactly what happens when Solomon is king. Solomon comes to the throne at a time when the nation is at its greatest strength following the reign of his father David—when the Israelites hold the most territory, when they are the strongest militarily and economically, when they are held in the highest esteem among the surrounding nations. But when they are at their greatest strength, Solomon marries unbelievers. And it happens—the nation is drawn away from God and torn apart:

> *King Solomon, however, loved many foreign women besides Pharaoh's daughter—Moabites, Ammonites, Edomites, Sidonians and Hittites. They were from nations about which the Lord had told the Israelites, "You must not intermarry with them, because they will surely turn your hearts after their gods." Nevertheless, Solomon held fast to them in love. He had seven hundred wives of royal birth and three hundred concubines, and his wives led him astray. As Solomon grew old, his wives*

*turned his heart after other gods, and his heart was not fully devoted
to the Lord his God, as the heart of David his father had been. He followed Ashtoreth the goddess of the Sidonians, and Molek the detestable
god of the Ammonites. So Solomon did evil in the eyes of the Lord; he
did not follow the Lord completely, as David his father had done.*

*On a hill east of Jerusalem, Solomon built a high place for Chemosh
the detestable god of Moab, and for Molek the detestable god of the Ammonites. He did the same for all his foreign wives, who burned incense
and offered sacrifices to their gods.*

*The Lord became angry with Solomon because his heart had turned
away from the Lord, the God of Israel, who had appeared to him twice.
Although he had forbidden Solomon to follow other gods, Solomon did
not keep the Lord's command. So the Lord said to Solomon, "Since this
is your attitude and you have not kept my covenant and my decrees,
which I commanded you, I will most certainly tear the kingdom away
from you and give it to one of your subordinates.* (1 Kings 11:1–11)

Because of his wives, Solomon is drawn away from the Lord, and the
kingdom is torn apart. Civil war splits Israel into two kingdoms, north and
south, but both kingdoms are so weak that foreign invaders soon come
in and take over. The northern kingdom disappears, ceasing to exist. The
southern kingdom becomes a puppet state of the Babylonian empire, and
thousands of its citizens are carried off to Babylon as hostages to discourage
any uprising.

Decades later, the hostages are allowed to return. But the land they
come back to is in ruins. Everywhere they look, buildings are torn down,
farmlands lie waste. God offers to help them rebuild under a leader named
Nehemiah. But as the reconstruction progresses, Nehemiah notices that
some of the returnees are again marrying unbelieving women in the area.
And he desperately pleads with them, "Don't do this. Don't marry unbelievers. This is what caused our problems in the first place."

*Moreover, in those days I saw men of Judah who had married women
from Ashdod, Ammon and Moab. Half of their children spoke the language of Ashdod or the language of one of the other peoples, and did not*

know how to speak the language of Judah. I rebuked them and called curses down on them. I beat some of the men and pulled out their hair. I made them take an oath in God's name and said: "You are not to give your daughters in marriage to their sons, nor are you to take their daughters in marriage for your sons or for yourselves. Was it not because of marriages like these that Solomon king of Israel sinned? Among the many nations there was no king like him. He was loved by his God, and God made him king over all Israel, but even he was led into sin by foreign women. Must we hear now that you too are doing all this terrible wickedness and are being unfaithful to our God by marrying foreign women?" (Neh. 13:23–27)

To marry an unbeliever is to be pulled away from God.

God has a plan, a blessing for our lives. He's revealed himself to us, and called us to an eternity with him. And his intention is for us to be part of what he's doing in the world. One of the firmest commitments we should have, therefore, is that if we marry, we will marry a believer. We will guard our walk with God by joining with someone who has the same eternal relationship to him that we have.

To marry an unbeliever is to marry someone whose values will pull you away from God.

On Sunday morning you'll want your family to join God's people—for worship, for fellowship, to be in touch with God and to hear his voice. But the unbeliever won't want to attend, and there'll be tension. And the temptation will be to give in to keep peace. To not go, and be drawn away from God.

You'll care about what activities your kids do and some of the places they go. You'll think about their friends and whom they date. You'll want to keep them from damage and sorrow, and from things that will deaden their spirit. But the unbeliever will see it differently. Where you see damage and sorrow, the unbeliever will see, "Well, that's what everybody's doing." Where you see danger in some of the places they go to and some of the activities they engage in, the unbeliever will see, "That's how you make connections to get ahead in life." And you're not in sync.

You'll want to give money to the Lord—to honor him, to help his work. The unbeliever will see this as a useless thing to do.

You'll want Christian friends, but the unbeliever won't take any pleasure in being around them. You won't be able to invite them over because the unbeliever won't cooperate. And if you go to their house, you'll go alone. Or, probably, you just won't go—it'll be too hard.

At the very center of life, your values and interests are different. You have different gods. Your God is the one who created you, the one who loves you, the one who saves you through Jesus Christ. The unbeliever's god is career, success, looks, entertainment, or making money.

To marry an unbeliever is to be drawn away from the goals God has for your life. But when we marry a believer, we guard and strengthen our walk with God, and we pursue his goals together.

One of the firmest commitments we should have is that if we marry, we marry a believer.

When Isaac said to Jacob, "Do not marry an unbeliever," he wasn't simply suggesting what he thought was a good idea. The Bible says he was commanding Jacob:

> So Isaac called for Jacob and blessed him. Then he commanded him: "Do not marry a Canaanite woman." (Gen. 28:1)

He *commanded* him. That is the strongest word the Bible has. That's the word the Bible uses for the Ten Commandments. That's how huge a matter it is in God's eyes.

If you marry, marry a believer.

6

A GOOD THING THE RIGHT WAY

Genesis 27:1–45

(Enter, wheeling a suitcase, and checking a boarding pass against an airport monitor.)

Fairbanks, Fairbanks . . . Fairbanks. Flight #782. Gate 12. Delayed, two hours. *(Grimace.)*

(To audience, referring to the suitcase) I think I blew it. You want a good thing . . . but maybe you don't get it the right way. I think I blew it, big time!

I wanted a good thing, a good thing. And I got it. You're looking at the future president and CEO of Energy Resources International.

My grandfather started the company in the 1950s. We were a small oil outfit headquartered in Dallas, drilling in central Texas. We did okay, competed with the big oil companies, found our niche in the market. But in the mid-'80s, my Dad saw the future—that the country was going to move away from oil dependency. So he talked my grandfather into turning the company toward solar energy—into developing a technology that would capture the sun's energy into small cells, which could then heat homes, power engines, run machines. And for the past thirty years we've been the leading developer in the field of solar technology. There isn't a competitor near us who knows as much as we do about harnessing this unlimited source of energy and making it affordable. We're the wave of the future. In the next decade we're projected to be a multi-billion dollar company. And the amazing thing is, we're still privately owned, a family company! You're looking at the next president and CEO.

I wanted a good thing. But the way I got it. . . . And now . . . *(motioning toward suitcases)*.

It wasn't the money. It wasn't the money that made me maneuver for the presidency. No, I wanted to be boss instead of my brother so that I could have control of the company, so that I could determine its future instead of him. I love the company . . . and he'd kill it if he were president. He doesn't understand the business. He doesn't have the discipline to sit at a desk and plan globally. If he became president, he would destroy the company.

Right now we're a company committed to Christian principles. We have a reputation for integrity. We have the potential not only to improve life in America, but to totally change life in the Third World, to reduce poverty in underdeveloped countries. We can protect natural resources and preserve the environment. We have an unlimited future to do good for the world community, and everybody in government and business knows it.

And it's all committed to God. Dad's always up-front about his faith in his business contacts or his meetings with foreign leaders. We contribute unbelievably to Christian organizations. Dad's on the board of two or three parachurch organizations, he's been an elder at church for twenty years, and a silent, generous giver year after year.

I want to continue all that, but my brother Eric wouldn't. Eric doesn't come to church. I doubt if he's a believer, and if he became president of the company all that would end—the giving to God's work, the Christian witness, the reputation for integrity. And he would kill the company, because he just doesn't have the temperament to run it. I had to have control of the company to keep all that from happening.

I wanted a good thing. I just wish I didn't have to do what I did to get it.

It should have been mine without my maneuvering to get it. Everything pointed to me. I don't know why Dad didn't see that. From day one, everything pointed to me. When we were born—Eric and I are twins; he's about two minutes older—my mom says that in the hospital when we were born, he came out and just sort of lay there, but when I came out I was wiggling and moving and reaching, as though I wanted to come out first. The nurses pointed to me and said, "This one has the energy; this one has the brains." From day one, it was obvious.

And then, when we were dedicated in church—I've seen the video: the pastor's holding both of us, we're about a year old, and Eric's bigger than I am; he's always been the bigger twin. He's just sitting there like a lump, blankly looking at the audience, while I'm exploring the pastor's lapel mic, trying to grab it. Typical.

But it's the pastor's prayer for each of us that gets you. I mean, the pastor doesn't know which one of us was born first, he's just praying as he senses a leading to do so, and he starts praying for me first. And he prays that I would *lead* the family for God, that I would continue the good name established by my father and grandfather, that I would be used as part of God's grace to the world, and that God would be honored in everything that I did. He prays for Eric too, but it's lesser stuff—that God would fashion his character, make him a source of joy to his parents and others—that kind of thing. But the leadership prayer—the *leadership* prayer—was for me. Everything pointed to me.

And Eric soon sensed it. Growing up, he was bigger and faster, but I was smarter. I was the one who always had the ideas, the schemes, the plans. During high school, while he partied, I ran student government. We both went to Baylor on scholarship—his was athletic, mine was academic. We joined the same fraternity, but had different roommates to get to know other people.

During our junior year we had the same Economics class. One night we were studying together for the final, and he just wasn't getting it. And he hadn't yet written his term paper. Two days before the final. I mean, he was going to flunk royally. He was so frustrated. I watched him read a page for the fourth time—no clue what it was saying. He leaned back *(blowing air out in frustration)* ...

I looked at him and said something I'd been planning for a long time. "Eric, why don't you let me take care of the business?"

"What do you mean?"

"The family business. Let me be president, let me run the company."

He thought we were having a casual conversation. "Yeah, sure, James, m'boy, you can run it. Maybe I'll just take the customers golfing."

"Promise me I can run it."

"You're serious, aren't you?"

"Yes."

"Well, why not? The way I'm partying, and the crowd I'm running with, shoot, man, I might not be alive in five years. And if I am, the last thing I want is to sit behind some desk staring at computer printouts. Tell you what—you write my Econ paper for me, and I'll let you run the company."

"You swear to it?"

"Yeah, I swear. I get a paper, you get to be president."

Everything pointed to me—the nurses, the pastor's prayer, even Eric's handing it over to me. I don't know why Dad didn't see it.

Well . . . I do know. Dad's a great guy, but he has a blind spot as far as Eric is concerned. And that's because Eric's been the athlete. And he's good, I admit that—all-state in high school, all-conference in college, played for the Cowboys for three years until he blew out his knee. He won the Super Bowl for them one year with an end-zone catch, two toes in, reaching high. He's on all the Cowboys highlight films. Dad has a blowup of the catch on the wall of his office at home. Eric was the golden boy growing up.

He and Dad used to go deer hunting—we own some property in south Texas. I went a few times when I was a kid. But I don't like to shoot things, so basically just the two of them went each year. They had a great time, became pals, and when Eric became a star athlete, Dad stayed just as proud of him as he could be. And he never could see that Eric didn't have the brains or character to run the company.

After Eric blew out his knee and couldn't play anymore, he came to work for the company. By then I had my MBA and was working in the different departments of the company to learn the business and get experience—research, product development and patents, marketing, legal, accounting, personnel—the whole company. Dad tried to plug Eric in the same way, but Eric couldn't focus. He wasn't disciplined. He couldn't sit at a desk and work. He was restless.

Finally, Eric found he could do halfway decently in sales. He could schmooze with the clients—took them golfing, just like he said. They always got him to tell stories about the Cowboys and about his famous catch. They would pose with him, and he would autograph the pictures for their kids. For a while he did okay in sales.

But after a while, even that sort of got old. It doesn't take too many years before you're yesterday's hero. By then the clients' kids had never heard of him, and the clients didn't care anymore. And it became more and more obvious that Eric wasn't contributing to the company. Even in sales, he always had to have an account representative with him to explain the products to the client and then to work out the details of the contract. It was getting obvious—who needs Eric?

His drinking increased. He started running with the Vegas crowd. Mom and Dad didn't know about his gambling. One time he begged me for some money because if he didn't pay off a debt pretty fast he'd be in trouble with certain people.

The thing that finally got Dad's attention a little was when Eric came back from Vegas one day with a wife. A wife! "Jodie." Some cocktail waitress he met and married on a weekend. I mean, talk about your bimbos—she probably inspired all the dumb blond jokes. You know—"Look, a dead bird." She looks up. "Where? Where?" We could always tell when she had been working on one of the office computers—there was white-out on the screen. One day she showed us a jigsaw puzzle she had finished—she was so proud she had finished it in only three months, because on the box cover it said "2–4 years."

I shouldn't make fun of her. Actually, Jodie's not as dumb as she looks. In fact, she saw where things were heading with Eric at the company—how he was getting more and more peripheral to the business. She began to get in his face about what was the future going to be. She told him that he'd better lock himself into some position or he could find himself out in the cold. And she began to play up to Dad, acting like Eric had good ideas for the company, putting it in Dad's head to turn the company over to him some day.

Mom was disgusted with her. Mom didn't like the way Jodie dressed. She didn't like her friends. She didn't like what she did with her days. She didn't like that Eric and Jodie never came to church. But mostly what worried Mom was that Jodie was trying to get Dad to turn the company over to Eric. Mom and I used to talk about it. Mom knew I should be president, but all the legal power to make it happen lay with Dad.

I used to hear my folks arguing. Mom would say, "Ike, you're blind as a bat. Don't you see what she's doing? If you give Eric control of the company, you're a stupid man."

"Becky, easy does it. All she's doing is looking out for her family. And Eric does have the name recognition that could help the company. He just might be the right one to be president. I haven't decided yet whom to turn it over to. Becky, I've built the business, and I think I can make a good decision about its future."

And that scared Mom. It became such an issue between her and Dad. Whenever they talked about company business, Mom would bring up the presidency and tell Dad he'd be a fool to name Eric. She harped on it so much that for several years Dad just stopped talking to her about company business. He kept his plans and his thoughts to himself.

Well, things came to a head two days ago.

For the past year the company's basically been treading water. Dad's eyes went bad. In fact, he's now legally blind. All he can make out is dark shapes. He doesn't go to the downtown office anymore. He tries to run the company from his office at home by telephone, and he gets Mom to read the mail and the faxes. So she was back in the loop again on company business, and she was jabbing him again about the future. But Dad just clammed up, and I could tell he was digging in his heels. I wished she'd back off; all she's doing is making him more stubborn.

When Dad's eyes went bad, he started putting on weight. He doesn't go out, he doesn't move around or exercise. He's put on a lot of weight—he's up close to three hundred pounds. I'm worried. At his age and weight he could have a stroke and go any moment. Mom's been worried too. Whenever she leaves his office after helping him with the mail, she's been secretly leaving the intercom open so she could hear from any other room in the house if he has a stroke and falls or calls.

Well, two days ago, she heard something over the intercom that horrified her. Dad was talking to Eric in his office. "Eric, I don't know how many years I have. At my age and weight . . . anyway, I've decided I need to put my personal and company affairs in order. Several years ago I had the lawyers draw up the papers for who would be the next president, but I left the names blank because I just hadn't made a final decision yet. But in the last couple of weeks I've made my decision—I'm going to turn the company over to you. I think you have a way with people that will be good for the company, and I'm going to put you in charge.

"I want the two of us to sign the papers. I haven't told your mother or brother about this. We don't need other witnesses because the lawyers have written it in such a way that just the two signatures by themselves are binding and irrevocable. Once we sign, it can never be changed. Not even I can change it. I had them write it that way so that if I'm disabled or incapacitated no one can get power of attorney and change what I want. Or if I die, no one can ever contest it in court. Once it's signed, it's forever.

"But I want to do the signing right, Eric. For old time's sake, I'd like to do it with memories of our good times. You remember how we used to hunt together, smoke the venison, and eat it? We haven't done that for years, and I can't do it now. But I'd like to bring back those memories as sort of a prelude to signing the papers.

"Eric, here's what I want you to do. Go to our place in south Texas where we used to hunt, bring back some venison, and smoke it like we used to. Let's have the biggest feast of meat and corn and coleslaw, and some of those hard rolls from Trader Joe's that I like. We'll remember the past, and then establish the future. Are you game?"

Was he ever! This was Eric's chance. He would never have to worry about a salary. He could get Jodie off his back. Surely there were people in the company who could make it work even if he didn't know what was going on. He jumped on it, told Dad what a great idea the "memory meal" was, and left that afternoon in his four-wheeler for south Texas.

Mom heard all this on the intercom, and immediately called me at our downtown office. She said she couldn't talk over the phone, but would come downtown and meet me for lunch.

At lunch, she told me the whole conversation Eric and Dad had, and said we had to do something to stop it. I said, "What could we do?" I was all for stopping it, but it looked like Dad had made up his mind, and if she hadn't changed it so far, she wasn't going to change it now. I told her, "You won't be able to change Dad's mind."

That's when I heard her plan.

"James, your dad is basically blind. He can't tell who's in the room with him. I can get smoked venison from Texas Country BBQ and fix it just the way your dad likes it. You take the venison into him, tell him you're Eric, eat the meal with him, and then sign *your* name to the papers. He won't figure out what's happening, and once the papers are signed, he won't be able to change it."

I couldn't believe what she was saying. I couldn't believe she would do that to Dad. My first thought was, "You're crazy, that's wrong." But I didn't say it—I didn't want to accuse her. Instead, I said, "Mom, it won't work. Dad will figure out I'm not Eric, and if he thinks I'm trying to take advantage of his blindness, he'll be furious. Instead of becoming president, he'll disown me entirely. It won't work, Mom."

I said that . . . but I hoped she'd have an answer, because I was ready to do almost anything. I wanted that presidency more than anything else, and it looked like it was slipping away from me.

Mom had an answer. "It *will* work. Look, Eric didn't take his hunting jacket with him. You wear the jacket when you go in. Your father will smell it. Make your voice sound like Eric—people are always getting you two mixed up over the phone anyway—and don't talk much. It'll work. Besides, we have no choice. If you don't do something, you'll lose everything."

So . . . last night, one day after Eric had left, I wheeled a cart into Dad's office at home.

"Dad."

"Yes . . . which son is it?"

"It's me, Eric. I've brought the venison, some corn and slaw, and the hard rolls from Trader Joe's. Let's have our meal and then sign the papers."

He didn't say anything. He just swiveled his chair toward me and looked at me. His eyes were cloudy and liquid, but he looked at me so steadily and directly that I couldn't believe he didn't see me as well as I saw him. I froze with terror. He knows! He can tell the difference in our voices!

"How did you get it so fast, Eric? Did you whistle and the deer came running toward you?"

"Dad, God was in it—I got a kill first thing this morning, about seven o'clock. It's a sign from God that this is his will."

At that moment I couldn't stand myself. I was ashamed of my father's blind spot toward Eric. I was ashamed of my mother's scheming. I was ashamed of my brother's worthlessness. And most of all, I was ashamed of my part in the whole sorry affair—wanting a good thing, but not getting it the right way. But it was like I was on a runaway horse, galloping wild. You can either hurl yourself off to your death, or you can hang on for dear life and ride out the madness to the end. I couldn't get off.

"It's a sign from God, Dad."

"Come here, Eric." He got up out of his chair. "A handshake is too formal for a father and son. Give me a hug instead. Come here."

Oh God, he suspects! I had no choice but to go give him a hug.

He buried his face in my neck and took a deep breath. When you can't see, you depend on hearing, on touch, on smell. His hearing was saying, "James," but his touch said, "Eric's hunting jacket, and the smell in the jacket is Eric too."

I hugged . . . and waited.

"Let's eat and sign, Eric."

(Letting out air in relief) Oh God, it's happening!

We ate and ate, until we couldn't put another bite down. We didn't talk much, and I was glad, for I was still unsure of my voice. Occasionally Dad mentioned some thoughts about the company, some ideas he had for the future. I just agreed with a grunt. I had so many ideas of my own for the company, but I had to pretend to be Eric grunting, "Uh-huh."

Finally, Dad said, "Time to sign."

He opened a drawer in his desk, brought out the papers, and spread them on the desk. I glanced through them—they were ironclad and comprehensive. "Full ownership of the company will be given to the son whose name appears below. "This son would have total control of all national and international operations, complete authority in all hiring and firing, including any decisions about relatives. The signatures would be binding and irrevocable.

There was a place to sign, and a line for the date. Dad asked me to put his hand and pen in the spot where he should sign, and I did. He wrote "Ike Abrams." In the place where he thought "Eric" would be written, I wrote "James Abrams."

"It's signed, Dad."

"Yes, Eric, it's done. And may God bless the world through the company and you."

"Eric, let me pray before you leave." And he prayed: for me, for the company, for the testimony to God that it could have. He prayed for new technology that would serve the world, for international success, and for a rich personal life for me and my family. He prayed for God's blessing on everything I would do.

As he prayed, a burning started inside of me. The longer he prayed, the fiercer became the burning. I knew it was God, but I didn't know whether God was saying my father's prayer would become true or whether he was saying I would pay a price for what I had done. I wanted a good thing, but I wasn't getting it the right way.

Finally, I got out of there. I ran out and saw Mom. She had heard it all on the intercom. I didn't say a word to her, but just threw Eric's jacket on the floor. I was heading for my car—I needed to get away from there. But just then Eric drove up, and that changed things. I didn't want him to see me. Mom grabbed his jacket off the floor, hung it up, and went upstairs. I disappeared into my old room.

From my window I saw Eric get out of his four-wheeler with plates covered with aluminum foil. He had the venison and everything else! Oh, no, he was going into Dad!

I listened at the intercom in my room. Apparently Dad was dozing in his chair after such a full meal, and Eric had to wake him.

"Dad, Dad, wake up, I'm back. I've brought the venison."

"Wha', wha', who is it?" I could tell Dad was confused. He was trying to wake up, trying to figure out who was talking to him and why someone was trying to feed him again, trying to figure out whether he had dreamed what had happened to him an hour earlier.

"Who is . . . what do you wa— . . . who are you?"

"It's me, Dad. Eric. I brought the venison . . . you wanted to sign the papers. . . . Dad, are you all right? Dad! Dad, are you all right? Dad, stop shaking. Stop shaking, Dad!"

I could hear the fear in Eric's voice, and I heard Mom upstairs start running to come down. She was scared Dad was having a stroke. I got ready to call 911.

But then Dad's voice was clear: "Eric, I just signed the papers. Look here on the desk. Tell me whose name is there." And I heard Eric spit out, "James! James, that son of a . . . ! James, James, I'll kill you for this. I swear to God, I'll kill you for this!

"Dad, this gives James everything. Everything! What do I get? Dad, can you do something? Something can be done, can't it?"

"Eric, I can't change it. It's unchangeable."

"Dad, please! Please! Dad, what am I going to do? What am I going to do?"

"Eric, I don't know what to say. You might try a legal challenge, but I don't think it will work. Maybe the best thing would be to move to another city, where you won't have to face it, see it, be reminded of it every day. Make another life for yourself. Maybe another country—maybe you and Jodie could open a club in Mexico somewhere. Eric, I don't know what else to tell you."

I snuck out of the house and went to my apartment.

This morning Mom called me at the office and said she was coming downtown to see me.

When she got there, she said, "Eric's going to kill you."

"Not really, Mom. He was just angry."

"That's what I thought too, at first," she said. But last night when I saw him come out of your father's office, the veins on his neck were bulging. I never saw such evil and hatred in his eyes before. He was still shouting he was going to kill you. But even then, I thought, 'He can't mean it, he'll calm down.'

"But this morning I got a call from Virginia. You know her, she's Tom's wife—Tom, the company attorney. Tom's probably Eric's best friend in the company. This morning they had their regular workout at the health club, and Eric told Tom what you did. And then he said, 'Tom, I'm going to tell you something—attorney-client privilege, Tom. My dad's going to die soon. And when he does, I'm going to kill James. I'll make it look like an accident, so that no one will know. But I'm telling you, Tom, so that somebody will know I didn't stand still for what he did.'"

"James, Tom probably did something he shouldn't have—I don't know the legalities—but he told Virginia, and Virginia called me a couple of hours ago. James, I'm afraid. Your dad doesn't look well; this hit him harder than I expected. I don't know what's going to happen, and I don't want you around. If your dad dies, and Eric does something to you, and they find out it was Eric who did it and put him away, then I'll have lost all three of you. And I don't want that to happen.

"Listen to me. My brother Leonard runs a crew on the Alaskan pipeline. Go up there, he'll give you a job. In a few months or a year, when things cool down, I'll e-mail or call, and you can come back. James, listen to me—you'd better get out of town right away."

Oh God, I wanted a good thing. But I didn't get it the right way. Everything pointed toward me—the nurses in the hospital, the pastor's prayer, my education, Eric's handing it over to me in college, my experience with the company, my ability. "God, you pointed everything toward its becoming mine. Would you have given it to me if I'd just waited?"

(Shuffling the suitcase in the direction of the gate) You want a good thing . . . a marriage, a child, a job, a house, a friend, a grade, a comfortable retirement. You want a good thing . . . .

(Looking at watch) My plane leaves for Fairbanks in an hour. . . . I didn't buy a return ticket.

7

UNEXPECTED, OVERWHELMING GRACE

Genesis 28:10–22

There are times when you may wonder whether God really does have a plan for your life. At one time you may have thought that he did, but things haven't turned out as you expected. You don't seem to be getting to where you thought you would get. And you wonder, "Did I miss it? Did I blow it?"

You chew over the past to see if there's some point where you got off track. Was it a decision you made? Was it something you said, something you did? You rehash the events. You replay the tapes in your mind. You see the faces, you hear the voices, and you second-guess yourself. "Is that where I lost it?"

You wonder about the past. You're uncertain about the future. "Am I drifting without direction? Am I still connected to some plan God has for me, or have I gotten off track with no way back?"

We're going to look at a man whose mind was churning with the same questions. He's afraid he's blown it in the past, and now, as a result, he's uncertain about the future. At one time he thought God had a plan for his life, but things haven't turned out as he expected. Has he lost what God intended for him?

The man's name is Jacob, and we're going to find him at a place he will later name Bethel. It's his second night out from his hometown of Beersheba. He's headed several hundred miles northeast to a community called Harran. He left Beersheba rather quickly, because his brother Esau would have killed him if he'd stayed. His brother had reason to be angry—Jacob had deceived their father Isaac into giving him an inheritance that rightfully belonged to Esau.

Isaac wasn't happy with what Jacob did, but he at least wanted him to be safe. And so he told Jacob to leave their home and go to another country, to a place called Harran, five hundred miles away, where they had relatives, and try to make a life for himself there—marry, have a family, and maybe one day, if things ever settle down and Esau feels differently, he can return.

Jacob's first day on the run, he moves as fast as he can—in case Esau has set out after him to catch him. And all that first day, he rehashes the past and second-guesses himself—"Should I have done what I did? Did I blow it?"

The second day, when it's apparent that Esau isn't on his tail, his thoughts turn to the future, to what's ahead, and he's scared. He's heading hundreds of miles to someplace he's never been. He doesn't even know if his relatives still live there—his family has had no contact with them for sixty years. They might be dead; they might have relocated. If they aren't there, he'll have no place to stay, no job, nobody. If they are there, will they welcome him, essentially a stranger, into their circle? "Get married and raise a family," his dad had said. What if there is no one there to marry? Where will that leave him?

He wonders about the past. He's uncertain about the future. He's afraid he's blown it.

He had thought that God had a special plan for his life—a plan to carry forward the family promises. Promises of inheriting a land—but here he is leaving the land, with the likelihood that he will never return. Promises of populating that land with generations of uncounted descendants—but here he is unmarried, with no descendants in view. Promises of becoming a people who would bless the world—but here he is heading toward some void that seems unconnected with any purpose he ever thought God had for his life.

It's his second night out, and the questions haunt him: "Does God still have a plan for my life, or have I lost it, blown it? Am I still connected to some plan God has for me, or have I gotten off track with no way back?"

To this man, and to us, God comes with unexpected and overwhelming grace. He comes at a moment we're not expecting him. He comes in a way we're not anticipating. He comes with a message of overwhelming grace to tell us that we've not blown his plan; his purposes for our life have not changed; he's still going to do everything he ever promised us.

We're going to be reminded of our God's unexpected and overwhelming grace, and we're going to find ourselves drawn even more deeply to him.

As the account opens, God comes to Jacob, unexpectedly, on his second night out. Jacob has put about fifty miles behind him, but he has hundreds to go. He's stopping for the night.

> *Jacob left Beersheba and set out for Harran. When he reached a certain place, he stopped for the night because the sun had set. Taking one of the stones there, he put it under his head and lay down to sleep.* (Gen. 28:10–11)

These words are setting us up for something unexpected that's going to happen. Jacob has "reached a certain place," he's arrived at a special place—a place where something's going to happen. The way verse 11 is written in the Hebrew language of the Old Testament, it creates a suspense and anticipation by mentioning "the place" three times. Here's how it reads in Hebrew:

> *When he reached a **certain place**, he stopped there, for the sun had set. Taking one of the stones from **that place**, he put it under his head, and he lay down to sleep in **that place**.*

Jacob has reached a place where something special is going to happen—a place where God is going to come to him, unexpectedly and with overwhelming grace.

And that's what happens. Unexpectedly, and to Jacob's great surprise, God comes to him.

> *He had a dream in which he saw a stairway resting on the earth, with its top reaching to heaven, and the angels of God were ascending and descending on it. There above it stood the Lord.* (Gen. 28:12–13a)

Again, the way this is written in Hebrew, it highlights Jacob's surprise and awe at what he sees in his dream. The Hebrew has explanation points as Jacob's eyes travel up this staircase, registering what he sees: "Look!" "Look!"

"Look!" The higher he goes, the shorter the sentences get, as he is increasingly stunned by what he sees. Here's how the Hebrew text becomes shorter and shorter, and increasingly more amazing:

He had a dream—

Look! A stairway resting on the earth, with its top reaching to heaven.

Look! The angels of God were ascending and descending on it.

Look! There above it stood the Lord.

As his gaze travels upwards, his eyes become wider, and his breath comes in shorter gasps—Look! God himself has unexpectedly come to him in this place.

He sees a stairway that connects heaven and earth. He sees the gateway or entrance portal between heaven and earth. God's messengers come down this entrance onto earth, and spread out to do God's work. Then they go back up through this gateway into heaven to report their activities. This place is the connecting point between heaven and earth.

The dream confirms to Jacob what he always knew—that this is the land that is central to God's purposes on earth, this is the land God will work through to bless the whole earth. This land, the land he fears he has forever forfeited because of his sin, the land he's now leaving, perhaps never to return. God has come to him unexpectedly, but the staircase simply reminds him of what he's lost, the plan he's blown—he's leaving God's chosen land.

But then, from the top of the staircase, God speaks to him. And the words are not words of judgment or rebuke. They are words of overwhelming grace—words that remind him of God's past promises; words that assure him that God will still make them true in Jacob's life; words that tell him that he hasn't blown God's plan for his life, that God's purposes for him haven't changed, that God will yet do everything he ever promised him.

There above it stood the Lord, and he said: "I am the Lord, the God of your father Abraham and the God of Isaac. I will give you and your descendants the land on which you are lying. Your descendants will be like the dust of the earth, and you will spread out to the west and to the east, to the north and to the south. All peoples on earth will be blessed through you and your offspring. I am with you and will watch over you wherever you go, and I will bring you back to this land. I will not leave you until I have done what I have promised you." (Gen. 28:13–15)

"Jacob, I'm going to give this land to you and your descendants. You haven't forfeited it. I'm going to bring you back to it.

"Jacob, I'm going to bring you back to this land with children—with descendants. You're going to marry in Harran. You're going to have children. And your descendants will multiply, and spread out in all directions on earth. And every person on earth will be blessed through you and your offspring.

"Jacob, you haven't blown my plan. You haven't lost it. My purposes for you haven't changed. I'm going to bring you back to this land, and through you and your descendants, I'm going to bless the earth.

"Moreover, Jacob, in the days ahead, I'm going to protect you. I'm going watch over you wherever you go. I'm going to be with you all the way until I've done everything that I've promised you.

"Jacob, my past promises are still in place, and the future is secure because I'll be with you wherever you go."

A message of overwhelming grace.

As Jacob wakes from his dream, he realizes that God has come to him at a desperate moment in his life—as he's spending his last night in the land, afraid that he'll never come back, afraid that he's blown God's plan forever. God has come to him in *this place* with an unexpected message of overwhelming grace.

*When Jacob awoke from his sleep, he thought, "Surely the Lord is in **this place**, and I was not aware of it." He was afraid and said, "How awesome is **this place**! This is none other than the house of God; this is the gate of heaven."* (Gen. 28:16–17)

This place is the gateway, the portal between heaven and earth. This is where God has entered into his life. This is a holy moment and a holy place.

He takes the large flat stone that was his pillow and turns it on end, so that it stands as a pillar, and he pours oil over it to make it glisten and to mark it as a holy spot.

Early the next morning Jacob took the stone he had placed under his head and set it up as a pillar and poured oil on top of it. He called that place Bethel, though the city used to be called Luz. (Gen. 28:18–19)

The stone will now serve as a historical marker to any traveler that something momentous happened in this place. And if Jacob ever returns, it will also mark the place where he will build a house of worship to God. And so he names that place *Bethel*, which in Hebrew means "house of God."

My friend, perhaps God will come to you in the same way—unexpectedly, at a time and place when you're not anticipating it. And he'll give you the same message of overwhelming grace—how much he loves you, and how he still has good plans for you.

It may be while you're driving to work, listening to a speaker or music on the radio or a CD. And through the words of the speaker, or the penetration of the song, God comforts your heart. He still has a good plan for you.

It may be the chance comment of a friend—someone who expresses some esteem for you, or affirms how God has used you in his life, or in the lives of others.

It may be when you're alone, on a quiet walk, or taking in some of God's creation, and your heart is lifted before him, and he draws you into his embrace.

An unexpected moment of overwhelming grace, when you realize nothing can stop his good plans for you.

And when you're overwhelmed with this unexpected grace, you find yourself responding as Jacob did—with a renewed commitment to him, with a deep desire to love and serve him in return.

Jacob's response is to offer God his life, his worship, and his service.

Then Jacob made a vow, saying, "If God will be with me and will watch over me on this journey I am taking and will give me food to eat and clothes to wear so that I return safely to my father's household, then the Lord will be my God and this stone that I have set up as a pillar will be God's house, and of all that you give me I will give you a tenth." (Gen. 28:20-22)

He binds himself to God with a vow, an oath. He will serve him for the rest of his life—"the Lord will be my God." He will build a place of worship to him on this spot—the stone pillar will become a house of worship, which he will financially support with a tithe, a tenth of all his income. Overwhelmed by God's unexpected grace, his gratitude shows in worship and giving.

Just as God's overwhelming grace came down that staircase to Jacob, so God's grace has come down to us through Jesus Christ. There was a moment in Jesus' life when he likened himself to Jacob's staircase. He was speaking with a man named Nathaniel, who would soon become one of his disciples. Nathaniel had heard about Jesus from another disciple, Philip. But Nathaniel was skeptical of what Philip was telling him, and decided he would have to see for himself. As he and Philip walked up to Jesus, Jesus suddenly stopped a conversation he was having, pointed to Nathaniel, and said to others standing around, "This man is no Jacob. There's no deceit or guile in this man, nothing false about him." Nathaniel did a double take—"How do you know anything about me?" Jesus said, "I know everything about you. I know that a few moments ago you were sitting under a fig tree, thinking about Jacob's staircase—about how God's grace came down to Jacob at that moment and in that place. Nathaniel, from now on, God's grace will come down to everyone through me."

Here's how the conversation is recorded in John 1:45–51:

> Philip found Nathanael and told him, "We have found the one Moses wrote about in the Law, and about whom the prophets also wrote—Jesus of Nazareth, the son of Joseph."
>
> "Nazareth! Can anything good come from there?" Nathanael asked.
>
> "Come and see," said Philip.
>
> When Jesus saw Nathanael approaching, he said of him, "Here truly is an Israelite in whom there is no deceit."
>
> "How do you know me?" Nathanael asked.
>
> Jesus answered, "I saw you while you were still under the fig tree before Philip called you."
>
> Then Nathanael declared, "Rabbi, you are the Son of God; you are the king of Israel."

Jesus said, "You believe because I told you I saw you under the fig tree. You will see greater things than that." He then added, "Very truly I tell you, you will see 'heaven open, and the angels of God ascending and descending on' the Son of Man."

My friend, heaven has opened, and God's overwhelming grace has come down to you through Jesus Christ. And when we are overwhelmed by God's unexpected grace, it shows in our worship and giving.

8

MATCHMAKER, MATCHMAKER

Genesis 29:1–14

One of the all-time great musicals is *Fiddler on the Roof,* the story of Tevye, a Jewish milkman living in Russia. He's caught between tradition and the social changes happening around him. In one of the songs in the musical, his three daughters sing to Yenta, the village matchmaker—a woman who kept a record in a book of all the village's eligible bachelors and available women, and was in business to "match" them, or bring them together. The girls sing to her:

> Matchmaker, matchmaker, make me a match,
> Find me a find, catch me a catch.
> Matchmaker, matchmaker, look through your book
>   and make me a perfect match.

"Make me a perfect match." That's not only a line in a musical, that's also the prayer of many a single person. "God, are you a matchmaker? Do you have a book? And if you do, do you have someone in mind for me? Someone perfectly suited to me? God, are you a matchmaker?"

From the passage we're going to look at, we're going to see that God's answer is yes. We're going to see that if God is calling you to marriage, then his plan for you is very specific, and, without fail, he will lead you to the one he has for you. If God is calling you to marriage, he will control the timing and sequence of events to bring you to the perfect match he intends for you. This means your dating can be without pressure or anxiety, and you can eventually enter marriage without doubt, without fear.

Now we need to be clear—God does not call everyone to marry. God fashions life for some so that their relationships are full and meaningful apart from marriage, their days are busy and productive, and they appreciate the freedom and richness of life God has given them. Some of you may sense that this is the life God has marked out for you, and if that is the case, you are joyful and content.

But others of you sense that God's plan for you is marriage. It hasn't happened yet. And maybe it won't happen in the next few months—you're not in a relationship that's moving toward that. But as best as you know, God has put this desire in you. And you often find yourself asking him, "God, do you have someone specific in mind for me?"

We're going to see from the life of Jacob that God's plan for you is very specific, and that, without fail, he will lead you to the one he has for you. We're going to see that if God is calling you to marriage, he will control the timing and sequence of events, and bring you to the perfect match he intends for you. You can date without pressure, and enter into the marriage without fear.

We're going to turn to a time in Jacob's life when he's in his early forties and not yet married. We know he's in his forties because the Bible tells us his twin brother Esau had recently, at age forty, married two pagan Hittite women, and that these marriages had brought grief to Isaac and Rebekah, his parents (Gen. 26:34–35).

The parents, partly to keep Jacob from a similar marriage to the pagans around them, but mostly to get him out of harm's way—because Esau was vowing to kill him for how he had tricked him out of the family blessing— tell Jacob to leave quickly for a distant land some five hundred miles away, and to go to a community called Harran, where their relatives were last known to live. He's to see if he can locate a man there named Laban—that's his mother's brother, his uncle. If he can find this man Laban and his family, perhaps he can stay with them. Maybe he can find a wife there, and begin to raise a family. And then someday, maybe, if things ever settle down, he can return back to his own land. But right now he must leave quickly, before Esau has a chance to kill him.

Jacob hurriedly throws a few things in a backpack and heads out.

His second night out, near the border between his country and the next, he's aware that he's leaving the land that is central to God's promises, maybe never to see it again. He's fearful of his brother and uncertain of what's ahead. He doesn't know where he's going; he's never been there before. He doesn't know where Harran is. He's afraid he could veer off a few degrees in any direction and totally miss it.

If he does manage to find Harran, he doesn't know if his relatives will still be there. It's been sixty years since they had any contact with them. They could have moved or died. He could get there and find them gone. If they are there, he doesn't know if they'll welcome him, or instead see him as a burden, another mouth to feed. Will they resent him, or be glad to see him? How long will he be able to stay with them?

As for a wife? Who knows if there's anyone there that he would want to marry, or who would want to share the uncertainties of his life?

On his second night out, he's fearful of his brother, sad for what he's leaving, and uncertain of what's ahead—uncertain whether God is still part of his life, whether God still has plans for him. As he finds a place to sleep before crossing the border, God comes to him in a dream and gives him a promise, a promise which includes marriage. God says, "Jacob, I'm going to be with you in the days ahead, and I'm going to bring you back to this land. And when I do, your descendants will multiply and be like the dust of the earth" (Gen. 28:13–15).

The last part—"your descendants"—is the promise of marriage. "Part of my plan for you," God says, "is that you will marry and have children, and your descendants will spread throughout the earth."

The dream tells him that God is calling him to marriage, and that in the days ahead God will control his movements—the timing and sequence of events—to make that marriage happen. God has called him to marriage, and God will lead him without fail to the one he has for him.

It's at this point that we pick up the story in Genesis 29:1:

Then Jacob continued on his journey and came to the land of the eastern peoples.

Hundreds of miles later—weeks, months later—he comes to a land that he only vaguely knows as "the land of the eastern peoples." That means he thinks he's on the right continent. For months he's been walking without a map—vague paths over hills, across empty stretches of land. Has he veered off by two degrees? By now he should be getting pretty close to the place he's looking for, but he's not sure. He thinks he's in the general area—the land of the eastern peoples—but he's uncertain. "God, am I in your plan? Are you in control?"

Yes, for as we'll see, God is controlling his movements. God is controlling the timing and the sequence of events.

As Jacob walks, uncertain, through the land, he spots a well, with three different flocks of sheep lying near it.

There he saw a well in the open country, with three flocks of sheep lying near it because the flocks were watered from that well. The stone over the mouth of the well was large. When all the flocks were gathered there, the shepherds would roll the stone away from the well's mouth and water the sheep. Then they would return the stone to its place over the mouth of the well. (Gen. 29:2–3)

The three shepherds in charge of the different flocks are sitting on the well, talking. They're probably young boys, for usually the youngest responsible person of the family was assigned to the sheep, to free the older ones for the heavy work. There's a large stone, like a flat boulder, covering the top of the well, designed to keep out blowing sand. But the three shepherds have made no move to take the stone off and get on with the business of watering their flocks. The three flocks are just

This strikes Jacob as strange. His first thought is, "Someone has not trained these boys well." Jacob is an experienced shepherd. He's just left his family's huge ranching operation. He knows you usually try to water sheep as fast as you can, and get them back onto the hills where they can graze some more and get fat and create wool. The economic profit in shepherding is in having well-fed sheep. Letting them lie idle on the barren area around the well is wasting time and money.

Seeing the boys sitting around talking strikes Jacob as strange, but it's none of his business. His immediate concern is: "Where am I?" The presence of the well and these shepherds tells him there's a settlement nearby. Maybe one of these boys or someone in the nearby settlement can give him directions to Harran, the place where his relatives were last known to live.

And so, he walks over to the shepherds and engages them in friendly conversation:

> Jacob asked the shepherds, "My brothers, where are you from?" "We're from Harran," they replied. (Gen. 29:4)

Harran! The nearby settlement is Harran, the very place he's looking for. God has led him over hundreds of miles, with no maps, exactly where he wanted to go.

But do his relatives still live in Harran, or have they long since moved and gone elsewhere? It's been sixty years.

> He said to them, "Do you know Laban, Nahor's grandson?" "Yes, we know him," they answered. (Gen. 29:5)

His relatives still live there. They're known in the community!

But what shape are they in financially? Would they welcome him, or see him as a burden? Are they on welfare, or do they have the financial wherewithal to host him? And so he asks, "Is the family economically okay? Are they in a good situation? Is it well with them?"

> Then Jacob asked them, "Is he well?" [Is he doing okay? Is he in the chips?] "Yes, he is, "they said," and here comes his daughter Rachel with the sheep." (Gen. 29:6)

"Oh, Laban's doing just fine. In fact, that's his daughter Rachel, coming with his sheep." And Jacob turns and sees in the distance a young woman, with a branch with leaves at the end of it, swishing along a flock of sheep, herding them toward the well and its water.

God is in control—controlling the movements of people, controlling the timing, controlling the sequence of events—bringing them together!

And so *(lilt, song)*, "some enchanted noon-time, he does sees a stranger, across an empty field." But instead of flying to her side, he has another idea: "How can I get rid of these shepherds?" She's heading in to get water at the well; two's company, five's more than a crowd. And so—kind of like a boyfriend who says to the kid brother, "Here's $10, go to the movies. Get lost, and leave me alone with your sister!"—he says, "Hey, you guys, water your flocks and get out of here."

> *"Look," he said, "the sun is still high* [there's a lot of daylight left]; *it is not time for the flocks to be gathered. Water the sheep and take them back to pasture."* (Gen. 29:7)

Now, all of a sudden, he takes an interest in their shepherding skills. Why don't they move the stone, water their flocks, get back to the hills . . . and leave him alone with this girl.

"We can't. The stone's too heavy for us. We need Rachel's help. That's why we've been waiting for her."

> *"We can't," they replied, "until all the flocks are gathered and the stone has been rolled away from the mouth of the well. Then we will water the sheep."* (Gen. 29:8)

The stone is too heavy for the three of them to lift. They need the strength of a fourth person, so they're waiting for Rachel to come.

The reason the stone was so heavy was because it wasn't just there to keep out sand. It also functioned as a lock on the well, to prevent unauthorized use of the water. In a land where water was scarce and valuable, all the wells were privately dug and owned. And a heavy stone cover was the equivalent of a good lock. It kept a shepherd from the other side of the hills, who wasn't entitled to the water, from taking what didn't belong to him. The stone was much too heavy for a single grown shepherd to lift it. Even these three young teenage boys couldn't lift it. That's why they were waiting for Rachel.

Every afternoon about this time, these four shepherds meet at the well in order to pool their strength, lift the stone, take the water they're entitled to, and then put the stone back. That's why they've been sitting around doing nothing—they're waiting for that fourth flock.

For the next ten to fifteen minutes, Jacob half-consciously engages in small talk with the shepherds. But he's watching this girl—they said her name was Rachel—he's watching her work the sheep closer and closer.

As Jacob watches her coming closer and closer, he's wondering more and more if God is doing exactly what he said he would do—leading him to his relatives and to *someone* among them whom he would marry.

By the time Rachel arrives at the well, settles her sheep down, and walks over to them, he's made up his mind—not just *someone*. Her! Because now he's gotten a good close-up look at her and at her sheep. She's a good-looking girl, and those sheep are in great shape! Well-tended, fat. The gal's a knock-out and a top-notch shepherdess to boot! She's got everything—beauty and brains, looks and talent. Bada-bing! Hubba-hubba!

And Jacob springs into action! He scoots the other shepherds off the well, gets his hands under that rock, and he lifts that huge stone off the mouth of the well and rolls it aside, briefly flexing his muscles.

He's showing off. He's just like a ten-year-old who's "popping a wheelie" in front of another fourth-grader. He's like a teenager showing off and get-ting the girl's attention. Then he asks, "Can I carry your books?" Only it comes out, "Can I water your sheep?"

While he was still talking with them, Rachel came with her father's sheep, for she was a shepherd. When Jacob saw Rachel daughter of his uncle Laban, and Laban's sheep, he went over and rolled the stone away from the mouth of the well and watered his uncle's sheep. (Gen. 29:9–10)

He draws a bucket of water from the well and takes it to some sheep to drink. Another bucket, to more sheep. Another and another and another, until all have drunk.

Rachel stands there, wide-eyed and amazed. What's going on? Who is this guy? She's never seen him before. He's bronzed tan by weeks in the sun, muscled and sweating. He's showing off to impress her, and doing a pretty good job of it. But she doesn't know why. Who is he, and why is he doing this? Why has he taken an interest in her?

When he's finished, and the other shepherds have gone, and it's only the two of them by the well, she learns the reason. He tells her he's a relative.

He's come hundreds of miles. For weeks he's been alone, on foot, uncertain, but trusting God was with him. He set out to find his relatives . . . and, his eyes say, to find her.

As Jacob pours out his story, gradually the stress and tension of weeks begin to leave him. His words eventually drift into silence. He isn't sure what else to say. He holds her by the shoulders and kisses her on each cheek, according to the custom, and then, suddenly, he finds himself uncontrollably sobbing. His long journey is over.

> *Then Jacob kissed Rachel and began to weep aloud. He had told Rachel that he was a relative of her father and a son of Rebekah. So she ran and told her father.* (Gen. 29:11–12)

Rachel tells him to stay there and watch her sheep, while she runs to find her father. Soon Laban arrives, and Jacob makes connection with the rest of the family.

> *As soon as Laban heard the news about Jacob, his sister's son, he hurried to meet him. He embraced him and kissed him and brought him to his home, and there Jacob told him all these things. Then Laban said to him, "You are my own flesh and blood."* (Gen. 29:13–14)

Laban's words—"You are my own flesh and blood"—in the Hebrew is literally, "You are bone of my bones and flesh of my flesh." This is only the second time these words appear in the book of Genesis. The first time was when God created Eve and brought her to Adam. Adam had seen all the animals paired up, but there was no one suited to him. But when God brought this one perfectly matched person to him, Adam said, "You are bone of my bones and flesh of my flesh. You are my own flesh and blood."

These closing words, echoing Adam's words to Eve, are a signal to us that God has led Jacob to the one perfectly matched to him, the one he would marry and have children with. God called him to marriage. God's plan was specific. And he controlled the timing and sequence of events to make it happen.

If God has called you to marriage, then he will lead you to the one he has for you. That means that if you're married, and you followed God in making that decision—you prayed for his guidance, you trusted his leading as you went into marriage—then you can look back and see the timing and events God used to bring you together. God moved one of you, then the other, then arranged the meeting, and got you together.

If you're married, God led you to each another, and joined you together. That's why we say at weddings, "What God has joined together, let no one separate." And that "no one" means you—don't you separate, don't *you* undo what God joined together. God's good future for you is through your marriage together. God's long-term blessings for you, the wonderful plans he has for you and your children, come through staying together, living through the disagreements, the frustrations, the hard stretches, the times when you drive each other crazy. Stay joined together, because God's perfect plan involves the two of you together.

If you're not married, but in your heart you believe this is God's intention for you, that he's calling you to it, then God's plans for you also are very specific. And he will control the timing and sequence of events, and without fail will bring you to the perfect match he has for you.

It might be in a night class at the university, a class you didn't intend to take—it isn't part of your major, but you need the units in order to keep your financial grant, and the class was offered at a time convenient to your work schedule. So you're taking this class just for the units. To you, it's a fluke, but not to God. God has his plan. During one of the class sessions you get into a back-and-forth exchange with the professor, and it involves a conflict or disagreement with your Christian faith. And you figure, "Hey, I'm never gonna take another class with this professor, and some TA is going to grade my final paper. I've got nothing to lose, so why not be totally up-front?" And so you speak out in some strong, clear, joyful way for the Lord. Afterward another student from the class is waiting by the door and says, "Hey, I really appreciated what you said. I feel the same way you do about that. I believe what you said." After talking outside the class for a few minutes, the two of you decide to go get coffee at the Student Union. And then you make a plan—let's say a date—to meet for dinner at the Student Union before the class next week. And then . . .

God is controlling the sequence of events, bringing you together.

It might be when you're on a business trip—some seminar or convention you're attending, some training session you're leading in another city. At the end of the day, a group of seven or eight of you go to dinner at a nearby restaurant. The waiter brings the orders and puts plates in front of everyone. Someone across the table, one of the group, someone who'd kind of caught your eye earlier in the day, very quietly and unobtrusively bows her head for a few brief seconds and silently thanks God for the food. And your eyes brighten and a private smile briefly crosses your face. After dinner, as you're paying your bill at the cash register, you mention to her that you appreciated seeing her do that. The next day at the conference, the two of you grab lunch together before going in for the afternoon sessions. You find out a little more about each other. You exchange business cards, and you start e-mailing. A couple of months later you have to return to the same city to lead another training session . . .

God is controlling the sequence of events, bringing you together.

It might be at church. One Sunday you see someone new sitting not too far away from you. When the service is over he seems uncertain what to do next. You go up to him and mention the refreshments, and you offer to get a cup of coffee for him. A brief conversation. He just moved here from Chicago to take a new job. He seems nice. A little more conversation with him . . . he *is* nice. You don't have any plans for lunch. Neither does he, and Applebee's is just down the street . . .

God is controlling the sequence of events, bringing you together.

My friend, if God has called you to marriage, he will control the timing and without fail will lead you to the one he has for you.

This means you can date without worrying, "Is this the one? Will I blow it? Will I do or say something stupid and lose this person?" You can relax, and let God work his plan.

You can date without pressure, and you can marry without fear—"Oh, God, will it be okay? Will it turn out all right? Will we do well together?"

Trust him. He's making a perfect match.

9

BROKEN BONES MENDING STRONGER

Genesis 29:14–30

Most of us, either while growing up or while raising a family, have to deal with broken bones at one time or another. I've had my share—a couple of broken arms over the years, a busted nose, an injury to my back. Nell and I have also had to deal with broken bones with three of our five kids.

Broken bones are initially painful. And then for months afterward, they're awkwardly in the way as you try to navigate life with a cast or crutches or physical therapy.

But the good thing about broken bones is that if you cooperate with the healing process, broken bones mend stronger. If you've ever seen X-rays of broken bones as they heal, you know that when they grow back together, they grow thicker at the spot of the break. The bone is actually larger and stronger in that area. But in order for this healing to take place, you have to cooperate with the process. You have to accept the heavy cast to start with, then maybe the lighter boot, and after that the physical therapy.

As you cooperate with the process, not only does the bone mend stronger, but sometimes other benefits or positive changes come into your life. We saw this with our daughter Mary. When she was a teenager, she had a severe break in her lower leg and was on crutches for a couple of months. All the adults stopped to talk to her about it, and Mary, who up until then had been rather shy and timid around adults, developed considerable confidence and poise in talking with them.

If you cooperate with the process, broken bones mend stronger, and good results come.

In the Bible, broken bones often speak of a broken life—of the pain and discipline that come from sin. After David committed adultery with

Bathsheba, he thought he had covered his tracks, and that no one knew about it. But during that time—when he was keeping everything secret inside him, stonewalling God—he felt like his bones were deteriorating. His joints ached. Everything was drying up and becoming parched inside. He later wrote:

> When I kept silent,
>> my bones wasted away
>> through my groaning all day long.
> For day and night
>> your hand was heavy upon me;
> my strength was sapped
>> as in the heat of summer. (Ps. 32:3–4)

All of the inward vitality of life was disappearing. Depression and heaviness were taking over. Life was wasting away.

And then it got worse for David. As he continued to keep his sin covered, as he refused to acknowledge it, he felt like his wasted bones were actually being crushed and broken. When he finally confessed and repented, he cried out to God, "Is there some way that the bones you have crushed can rejoice?"

> Let me hear joy and gladness;
>> let the bones you have crushed rejoice.
> Hide your face from my sins
>> and blot out all my iniquity. (Ps. 51:8–9)

"Can the broken bones be healed so that once again my life is joyful? God, can you mend my life? Can you put it back together again?" And the answer is, "Yes." As David submits, there's a process that will bring healing.

The wonderful thing about God's love is that the same thing is true in our lives. There may be some area of sin in our lives—some issue that we don't even want to think about. We ignore it; we pretend it's not there. But even as we block it out, its effects begin to wear on us. The vitality and joy of life disappear. There's a brittleness to life, depression and heaviness set in, and we seem to be drying up. But if we submit to what God is doing, if we cooperate with his process of healing, broken lives—like broken bones—mend stronger, and God uses the experience to bring good.

In Middle Eastern countries, a shepherd would sometimes have to sorrowfully break the bone of a disobedient sheep, a sheep that simply would not stay with the flock, but would always wander away. Because of the broken bone, the shepherd would then have to carry the sheep wherever it went. And during the healing process, as the shepherd carried the sheep, the sheep would grow close to the shepherd. Then, when the bone was mended, the sheep would easily follow the shepherd where he led. Broken bones mend stronger, and good results come.

Maybe today something like that can happen between you and your God. A time when you can admit the pain and the brokenness, and can begin the process of healing. And God's promise to you is: broken bones mend stronger, and good results come.

We see this happening in the life of Jacob. There's an issue of sin in his life that he's never faced up to. All his life he's schemed and maneuvered to get what he wants. He deceived his blind father into giving him a blessing intended for his older brother. By concealing his identity, he managed to get his father to transfer the family promises to him.

But the consequences threw his life into turmoil. Life started breaking apart. As we've seen, his brother swore he would kill him if he could get his hands on him. So his mother said, "You've got to leave. Go to my brother Laban five hundred miles away. Stay with him for a while, and if your brother ever gets over his anger, we'll let you know if you can return."

After months of travel, Jacob arrives at his destination, and surprisingly finds the relatives he's looking for. Even more, one of his uncle's daughters is extremely beautiful, and captures his heart. It looks like God's being good to him, and that he won't have to face up to his sin.

But the path of sin never leads to blessing. So God must bring Jacob's sin before him so that he can see it for what it is, and turn from it. The result will be more brokenness in Jacob's life. But as Jacob submits to God's process, he will find God healing his brokenness, mending his life in order to carry his promises forward. And like the sheep carried by the shepherd through healing, Jacob's life becomes even more blessed than he expected.

We pick up the account where it seems that Jacob can go on in life without facing his sin. He's found his relatives; he's living with his uncle Laban;

he's smitten with Laban's youngest daughter Rachel. His uncle has said to him, "You are my flesh and blood," the same phrase Adam had said when introduced to Eve, which means his uncle is expecting there will be a marriage in the future. Since then he and his uncle have actually agreed on a date for the wedding. Things are looking good. Jacob doesn't have to think about his sin. This is the picture as we turn to Genesis 29.

> After Jacob had stayed with him for a whole month, Laban said to him, "Just because you are a relative of mine, should you work for me for nothing? Tell me what your wages should be."
>
> Now Laban had two daughters; the name of the older [literally, "the big sister"] was Leah, and the name of the younger [literally, "the little sister"] was Rachel. Leah had weak eyes, but Rachel had a lovely figure and was beautiful. Jacob was in love with Rachel and said, "I'll work for you seven years in return for your younger daughter Rachel."
>
> Laban said, "It's better that I give her to you than to some other man. Stay here with me." So Jacob served seven years to get Rachel, but they seemed like only a few days to him because of his love for her.
>
> Then Jacob said to Laban, "Give me my wife. My time is completed, and I want to make love to her." (Gen. 29:14b–21)

Jacob stays with Laban for a month. During this time he apparently earns his keep, working simply for room and board, but no salary. He helps with the flocks, builds stone walls, fixes things in the household.

Laban notices that Jacob is a diligent and competent worker—energetic, skillful, and multi-talented, which should be no surprise considering the vast ranching operation he left when he fled his homeland.

Laban also notices how Jacob keeps looking at his youngest daughter Rachel. He notices how much time he spends talking with her.

Laban has two daughters. The older one, Leah—well, she has *weak eyes,* which may mean that her vision is poor, but more probably means that her eyes are dull and listless, without the sparkle and luster that was prized as a mark of beauty in that time.

But apparently Leah suffers in comparison with her younger sister in other ways also. Evidently Leah is a rather plain or dowdy woman, because in contrast, Rachel is described as having a lovely figure and a beautiful face. And the truth is, Jacob was in love with Rachel.

So one day, Laban—after about a month, realizing he has a good worker in Jacob whom he doesn't want to lose, and noticing Jacob's attentiveness to Rachel—very shrewdly says to Jacob, "Jacob, you ought to make a little more than just room and board for the good work you're doing. I appreciate that you're a relative, you're family. But at the same time you shouldn't work for me for nothing. Is there some salary I can pay you so that you would stay here for a while? Tell me what wages you would want."

Now this sounds like a wonderfully generous offer that Laban is making. But in reality Laban is shrewd and smart—every bit Jacob's equal in conniving, maneuvering, and manipulating. His offer sounds generous and open-handed, but in reality Laban has figured out a way to get years of free work out of Jacob. He knows Jacob would like to marry his daughter Rachel. He also knows Jacob doesn't have the customary bride price to offer the father. All Jacob has to offer is more labor.

And sure enough, Jacob comes back as Laban expected: "Jacob was in love with Rachel and said, 'I'll work for you seven years in return for your younger daughter Rachel.'"

The custom of the day was that when you proposed, you didn't give an expensive ring to the girl. Instead you gave an expensive present to her father—a bride price. This was to compensate him for the pain of losing his precious treasure. The presents were so large that daughters were actually the chief source of wealth for a family.

It was a wonderful custom. I've often regretted we don't have the same custom in our culture. As a father of three beautiful daughters, rather than getting great sums to marry them, I gave great sums to marry them!

Jacob's problem is that he doesn't have any money to give Laban. He doesn't have an appropriate bride price to pay for Rachel. All he has to offer is the equivalent in labor. And so he offers the rather extravagant gift of seven years' free labor. This is a large bride price to suggest—but this is a beautiful girl, for whom others would offer Laban a fortune, and Jacob doesn't want to take a chance of being outbid.

Laban is pleased. He gets a prize worker for free for seven years, and he has to admit the man is good husband material anyway—capable, smart, and strong. Better to marry his daughter to someone like him rather than to some Joe Blow in the community. And so he agrees, "It's better that I give her to you than to some other man. Stay here with me." Work for me seven years and you can marry my daughter.

So great was Jacob's love for Rachel, and so thrilled was he that there was a way he could offer an equivalent fortune for her, that the seven years seemed to fly by like only a few days. And at the end of the time he comes to Laban and says eagerly, "The seven years are over. Let's set a wedding date."

Things are looking good for Jacob. He's going to get married and have a family. He hasn't had to think about what he did back in Canaan—deceiving his blind father, cheating his older brother out of an inheritance. It's as though the past never happened.

But in the midst of this rosy picture, the Bible quietly clues us that God hasn't forgotten the past or Jacob's sin. There's a small phrase in the midst of this bliss that reminds us of the past, and lets us know that God is going to force Jacob to come to grips with it. It's the small phrase in verse 20: "only a few days."

> So Jacob served seven years to get Rachel, but they seemed like only a
> few days to him because of his love for her.

The Hebrew phrase, translated here as "only a few days," is translated as "for a while" in the passage where Jacob's mother spoke to him when he left them seven years earlier: "Flee at once to my brother Laban in Harran. Stay with him for a while until your brother's fury subsides" (Gen. 27:43–44).

Stay with him "for a while," a few days, until Esau's anger passes. It's now been "a while." The seven years, which seem like just a short while to Jacob, are now enough that Esau's fury has subsided. As far as Esau and the parents are concerned, it's okay for Jacob to now return home. But as far as God is concerned, it's not okay. Jacob's not yet ready for God to work his good promises in him. God must keep Jacob right there in Harran until he faces his sin and acknowledges it.

God is unwavering in his commitment to be good to us. His intention to bless us is unchanging. But first he will address whatever sin there is in our life. He'll confront us with it, and wait until we deal with it, before he carries out his good purposes for us.

And so, in the verses that follow, we see how God confronts us with our sin. If necessary, the bones are broken in order that God can draw us to himself. He forces us to see our sin for what it is. He puts it in front of us, exactly as it is, and asks us to admit it, to acknowledge what we've done. For he has to heal our brokenness before he can continue his blessing.

In the verses that follow, God brings further breaking and crushing into Jacob's life, confronting him with his sin—the sin of deception—as Laban does exactly to him what he did to Esau. Just as Jacob concealed his identity to deceive his father's darkened eyes in order to take something from the firstborn, so Laban will conceal an identity in the dark to deceive Jacob in order to gain something for the firstborn. God is forcing Jacob to look at his sin.

> So Laban brought together all the people of the place and gave a feast. But when evening came, he took his daughter Leah and gave her to Jacob, and Jacob made love to her. And Laban gave his servant Zilpah to his daughter as her attendant.
>
> When morning came, there was Leah! So Jacob said to Laban, "What is this you have done to me? I served you for Rachel, didn't I? Why have you deceived me?"
>
> Laban replied, "It is not our custom here to give the younger daughter in marriage before the older one. Finish this daughter's bridal week; then we will give you the younger one also, in return for another seven years of work." (Gen. 29:22–27)

The wedding has arrived. The community is invited for a week of feasting to celebrate. During the seven days there will be dancing, races, and huge meals. About the middle of the week, the actual wedding ceremony will take place, and then the celebrating and eating will continue for another three to four days.

The day of the wedding, the bride is be kept from view, similar to our custom where the groom often doesn't see his bride before the wedding ceremony. That evening, before the wedding, the male guests gather separately for a huge feast. Some distance away, off by itself, away from all the activities taking place, is a special tent—the bridal suite, prepared and ready for the bride and groom later that evening. A torch at the entrance to the tent lights the path to it. While the men eat and drink and dance, Jacob keeps looking at that special tent, and then turns in the other direction to look at the tents where the women and his bride are, impatient for everyone to hurry up and get this meal and ceremony over!

Finally, his father-in-law Laban makes the necessary speeches and toasts, and then offers to lead Jacob to the bridal tent. The other men laugh and make jokes, but Jacob doesn't care. He hardly hears them. He follows his father-in-law into the bridal tent. By the light of the torch outside, he sees the flowers, the cushions and the pillows inside the tent.

His father-in-law leaves him, and Jacob lies on one of the cushions, waiting. More songs go on outside. Finally he hears the voices of the women—they're escorting his bride from the tents of the women. He knows his bride is heavily veiled, hooded, so that no other man can look on her as she comes to him. The women are singing and dancing as they come. It seems to take them forever to get there.

He hears the procession of women passing the campfire and the banquet tables where the men are, making their way toward his tent. Finally, he sees shadows approaching his tent flap. They pull it aside, and his veiled, hooded bride steps through the opening.

The outside torch is extinguished. And now, inside the tent, there is blackness, the blackness of a night where the clouds have shut all light from moon and stars, and where the skins of a tent have shut out any remaining glow from a dying fire. It's a blackness where only fingers and lips and whispers communicate, a blackness that draws its secrets around the love and passion of the night.

But in the morning, when he can finally see his bride—it's Leah! It's Leah! It's not Rachel! He stumbles out of the tent, trying to clear his head, trying to make sense of what happened. "Laaaban! Laban, where are you?"

He begins to run through the camp, looking in tents to find Laban. Finally he spots him, maybe sitting on a rock on the edge of the camp. Laban knows that Jacob will be looking for him, and he's placed himself at a spot away from the traffic and hearing of others.

Jacob runs to him, and with anger and fury shouts, "How could you do this to me? How could you? I put in seven years for Rachel. Why have you done this to me? Why have you *deceived* me?"

In pain and anguish, he's looking for some explanation for this monstrous trick that has broken his life apart and ruined all his plans and hopes.

As he stands there dazed and confused before Laban, we begin to quietly hear the voice of God. "Jacob, do you now see *your* sin? Jacob, you must look at your sin. You must acknowledge it; you must admit it; you must deal with it, so that we can move forward to the good plans I have for you."

We hear the voice of God, quietly. It comes through in two ways in these verses. First of all, it comes through in Jacob's cry, "Why have you deceived me?"

This is exactly what he had done to his father and his brother—he had *deceived* them. When Esau returned to his father Isaac with the venison, expecting the blessing, he learned that Jacob had already been there, concealing his identity, and deceiving his father in the darkness of his blind eyes. And the language of that event more than seven years earlier now comes back to confront Jacob with his own sin.

> [Esau] *said to his father, "Bless me—me too, my father!" But he said, "Your brother came deceitfully and took your blessing." Esau said, "Isn't he rightly named Jacob? This is the second time he has taken advantage of me* [literally, "he has deceived me"]: *He took my birthright, and now he's taken my blessing!"* (Gen. 27:34b–36a)

And the voice of God quietly says to Jacob, "Jacob, do you hear what you are saying, accusing Laban of deceiving you? Do you hear the words you are using? Laban concealed an identity to deceive you in the darkness. Jacob, you did the same thing—you concealed your identity to deceive your father in his darkness."

The second way God's voice comes through to Jacob is in how Laban answers him. When Jacob cries, "Why have you done this to me? Why have you deceived me?" Laban replies, "It is not our custom here to give the younger daughter in marriage before the older one."

"That's not the way we do things around here—we don't do something for the younger ahead of the older." The younger does not come ahead of the firstborn. And in Laban's words, Jacob hears his sin—he, the younger, has gone ahead of his older brother.

Up to now, Jacob has refused to think of those words—*younger, older*. He's blocked those words from his mind as he's been ignoring his sin. When he talked with Laban about wanting to marry one of his daughters, he didn't use the language of younger and older. He avoided those words. In the Hebrew, he used different words—instead of younger and older, he used the Hebrew words for "little sister" and "big sister":

Now Laban had two daughters; the name of the older ["big sister"] *was Leah, and the name of the younger* ["little sister"] *was Rachel. Leah had weak eyes, but Rachel had a lovely figure, and was beautiful. Jacob was in love with Rachel and said, "I'll work for you seven years in return for your younger daughter* ["little sister"] *Rachel.* (Gen. 29:16–18)

But now, in the words of Laban, God is forcing Jacob to face the actual words of his sin. Laban uses the words Jacob has not yet faced up to—the younger does not come ahead of the firstborn.

God is confronting Jacob with his sin. "Jacob, your father Isaac could not see. He didn't know that the younger was being substituted for the firstborn. And now when you could not see, you did not now that the firstborn was being substituted for the younger. You took advantage of the darkness of your father's sight to conceal your identity and deceive him. Another took advantage of the darkness of your night to conceal an identity and deceive you. Jacob, do you see your sin?"

My friend, God's voice will speak to us of our sin. Sometimes through pain, through anguish, as though life is breaking apart. And the question is: Will we submit to him, and will we allow him to begin the process of healing?

Jacob does—he hears God's voice, he recognizes his sin, and he submits to God's healing in his life. He will stay another seven years. And good results will come. He accepts God's discipline, he yields to God's correction, and he will find himself blessed even more than he could have imagined. God is preparing to bless him with sons and daughters beyond expectation through two wives and their servant girls. That's the meaning of verses 27–30:

"Finish this daughter's bridal week; then we will give you the younger one also, in return for another seven years of work."

And Jacob did so. He finished the week with Leah, and then Laban gave him his daughter Rachel to be his wife. Laban gave his servant girl Bilhah to his daughter Rachel as her attendant. Jacob made love to Rachel also, and his love for Rachel was greater than his love for Leah. And he worked for Laban another seven years.

Laban asks Jacob to wait until the end of the week's ceremonies for Leah, and then he will also give him Rachael as a wife, if Jacob promises him another seven years of free labor.

Things are not happening the way Jacob expected. But he submits to the healing process. And within the culture and customs of the day, God is getting ready to bless him with sons and daughters beyond expectation. The biblical author is preparing us for the good results.

The passage mentions that Laban gave a servant girl—a personal maid—to each of his daughters. The servant given to Leah is mentioned in verse 24, and the servant given to Rachel is mentioned in verse 29. According to the culture of the day, these maids become the personal property of the two daughters.

In the next section of Scripture, the two wives, Leah and Rachel, will start competing with each other to present Jacob with sons and daughters. The tensions and rivalry will pull their two personal maids into the contest to see which wife and maid can produce the most children. And by the end of the next section, we'll see a dozen little children, God's blessing, running around all over the place. Far beyond anything Jacob expected.

My friend, God's commitment to you is unwavering. His intention to bless you is unchangeable. But he will ask you to face your sin and turn from it, in order that he can move his good purposes ahead for you. Submit to his correction, and let the process of healing begin. Broken bones always mend stronger, and good results come.

10

THE PROMISE ALL OVER THE PLACE

Genesis 29:31–30:24

Two businessmen were meeting for lunch. Their conversation covered world events, competition, taxes, regulations, and the cost of living. Eventually they got around to talking about their families. One man said, rather proudly, "I have six children." The other man sighed wistfully, "That's a nice family. I wish I had six children." The first man answered, sympathetically, "Oh, don't you have any children?" "Oh, yes, I have twelve. I wish I had six."

We're going to look at a man who has twelve children. And he's absolutely delighted he has twelve, for to him they represent the unbelievable promise of God.

Some people may call their children "Eenie," "Meenie," and "Miney" because there ain't gonna be no "Mo," but not him. Instead, as he looked at his twelve children, all born within a seven-year period, and said, "As I live and breed," he knew that every one of them was proof that God was making good on his promise to him.

This man is Jacob, and God's great promise to him is that he would have descendants as thick as the dust of the earth—that his children would multiply over generations into a nation that would bless the world more than any nation.

Even before he was born, he had this promise from God—that he would have innumerable descendants. You'll remember that when his mother was pregnant with him and his twin brother, and when she wondered why there was so much turbulence in her womb, God's answer was: *Two nations are in your womb*—two nations!—*and two peoples from within you will be separated* (Gen. 25:23a). From birth, the promise was that a nation would come from him.

Then when he fled his homeland to escape his brother's fury, before he left, his blind father blessed him, and his father's blessing repeated the promise:

> *May God Almighty bless you and make you fruitful and increase your numbers until you become a community of peoples.* (Gen. 28:3)

As he was fleeing the land, the second night out, before he crossed the border, heading five hundred miles to a place he'd never been to find some relatives he'd never seen, God's promise came to him a third time:

> *Your descendants will be like the dust of the earth, and you will spread out to the west and to the east, to the north and to the south. All peoples on earth will be blessed through you and your offspring.* (Gen. 28:14)

Now God is making good on this promise, as child after child after child is born to him.

Everything in Jacob's life has been moving toward the birth of these children, and everything that follows will flow from it. The Scripture makes this clear—that these births are the highlight, the center point of his life—by arranging all the episodes of his life in a chiastic pattern, where everything moves toward these births and then everything flows from them:

Promise given, family scheming	*(25:19-35)*
Deception and strife with foreigners	*(26:1-35)*
Blessing stolen, flight from land	*(27:1-28:9)*
Encounter with God: dream	*(28:10-22)*
Arrival at Laban's	*(29:1-14)*
Deception about wages	*(29:15-30)*
Birth of the children	***(29:31-30:24)***
Wealth through wages	*(30:25-43)*
Departure from Laban's	*(31:1-55)*
Encounter with God: wrestling	*(32:1-32)*
Blessings replaced, return to land	*(33:1-20)*
Deception and strife with foreigners	*(34:1-31)*
Promise renewed, family scheming	*(35:1-29)*

In a chiasm, the top and bottom units match each other as they head toward the center. The center is the heart, the main thrust that everything is pointing to. These children are God's promise all over the place.

The purpose in all of this is for us to see that God will fulfill his good intentions for us, too. God will follow through on his good plans for our life.

And as we trace the sequential births in this section, we'll see that God will fulfill his good intentions despite the sorrows we've experienced—sorrows of loneliness, sorrows of being unappreciated, resented, treated unfairly, sorrows of being made to feel we don't fit in.

We'll also see that God will work his goodness despite the strife we've faced—despite the times we've been attacked and found ourselves lashing back, despite the angry frustration we've felt, despite the bickering and jealousy and conflict we've endured.

And finally, we'll see that God will fulfill his good intentions despite our small obedience—an obedience that is often so imperfect, so faulty, so feeble. Yet God's commitment never wavers.

Despite our sorrows and strife and small obedience, God is putting together the pieces of his plan, moving us toward his good promise.

The events of this section are messy. It's full of bickering and envy, favoritism and conflict, jealousy and jabs. And all this messiness and frustration and friction shows up in the names that the children are given. But through all the sorrows and strife and small obedience, God is building the family, giving shape to the twelve tribes of Israel—forming the nation that will bless the world.

Your life, too, may seem messy and disjointed, but God knows the good plans he has for you, and he's taking you there. Just as he was working his plan at the center point, the highlight of Jacob's life.

First we see that even in the midst of sorrow, God is fulfilling his good plan. We read of a woman who lives with sorrow and heaviness. She's unloved, unappreciated, isolated, alone. Through no fault of her own she finds herself resented, treated unfairly. And as she bears children, the names she gives them reflect her sorrow. But in the midst of her sorrow, God is working his good plan.

When the Lord saw that Leah was not loved, he enabled her to conceive, but Rachel remained childless. Leah became pregnant and gave birth to a son. She named him Reuben, for she said, "It is because the Lord has seen my misery. Surely my husband will love me now." (Gen. 29:31–32)

Leah knows she's unloved. Jacob never wanted to marry her. He was tricked into having her. But since she is his wife, he has certain husbandly duties or responsibilities that he owes her, and so he fulfills them. But he takes no pleasure in her company. And apart from those relatively infrequent nights, he spends almost no time with her. She's alone—isolated, unappreciated.

And in sorrow she names her first son *Reuben*, which literally means, "Look, a son!" But the name Reuben also sounds like the Hebrew for "misery"—*ra-be-an*, "He has seen my misery." It also sounds a bit like the Hebrew for "love"—*eha-bon*, "He will love me now." And so she names her son with the hope that maybe now her husband's heart will turn toward her—"God has seen my sorrow; surely my husband will love me now, for I have borne him a son."

But it doesn't happen. There's still no love between them. Her sorrow continues. She prays for God to give her another son—perhaps that will make a difference. When another son comes, she names him Simeon—"One who hears."

> *She conceived again, and when she gave birth to a son she said, "Because the Lord heard that I am not loved, he gave me this one too." So she named him Simeon.* (Gen. 29:33)

"God has heard my prayer. God gave me another son. Maybe now my husband will love me."

But again it seems to make no difference in the relationship—there's still no warmth, no affection. Surely if a third son is born she'll be appreciated, valued, honored. Surely three sons will attach her husband to her.

> *Again she conceived, and when she gave birth to a son she said, "Now at last my husband will become attached to me, because I have borne him three sons." So he was named Levi.* (Gen. 29:34)

Levi sounds like the Hebrew word that means "attached."

But again it doesn't happen. And Leah becomes resigned to her sorrow. She realizes nothing she does will endear her husband to her. Her only comfort is in the Lord. The Lord has been good to her—the Lord has loved her, giving her sons. Somehow God is working good in her life apart from the human longing and loneliness she feels. And she will praise him. And so, when the fourth son is born, she names him Judah—"Praise."

> *She conceived again, and when she gave birth to a son she said, "This time I will praise the Lord." So she named him Judah. Then she stopped having children.* (Gen. 29:35)

Like Leah, you also may be living with ongoing sorrow—perhaps unloved, unvalued, wondering where you fit in. Through no fault of your own you may feel resented, shut out, on the fringe. And you wonder if God knows the longing of your heart to be loved and accepted. And God says to you that in the midst of your sorrow and heaviness, though you may not yet see it, he is adding his pieces to his good plan for you.

(A few pieces of a puzzle—different geometric shapes— appear scattered on a screen.)

God works his good plan despite the sorrows we've experienced.

And God works his goodness despite the strife we've faced. Despite the times we've been attacked and have lashed back, despite the bickering and jealousy and conflict we've endured, despite the angry frustration we've felt, God works his good plans for us.

In the next section we see God working his good purposes despite strife and friction in the family. It's a hornet's nest of rivalry and competition and one-upmanship. It's a battle of wills and wombs. And the names of the children reflect the jabs and barbs of people who have become so bitter against one another that they've shut God out of the picture. In their desire to hurt one another, they search for ways to force things to go their way, and in the process God is pushed to the periphery.

In the previous set of verses (Gen. 29:31–35), God was prominent in Leah's sorrow. Four times in her heaviness she calls him by name—his personal, intimate name—the Lord, *Yahweh* in Hebrew. Leah clings to him in her sorrow:

> *When the Lord saw that Leah was not loved, he enabled her to conceive. . . . She named him Reuben, for she said, "It is because the Lord has seen my misery."*
>
> *She conceived again, and . . . she said, "Because the Lord heard that I am not loved, he gave me this one too."*
>
> *She conceived again, and . . . she said, "This time I will praise the Lord."*

But as we move into the next section (Gen. 30:1–13) of strife and conflict, attack and competition, the Lord's personal name disappears, and instead he becomes some distant, impersonal force—a means of power over others, a weapon to use against others, but not one who shares your sorrow and hurt. Instead of finding the personal intimate name of *Yahweh*, we find *Elohim*—"God"—a more impersonal word for a distant deity, a supreme being. The people in the story no longer call on the name of a loving, personal, intimate God. Instead they simply see him as a powerful ally who will serve their vengeful agenda.

And yet, in the midst of all the competition, backbiting and friction, unknown to the people involved, the Lord is still working his good plans. Despite the strife we face, he moves his good purposes forward. More children come.

Rachel sees her sister Leah give birth to four sons, one right after another, while she is unable to conceive. And the pain of being childless is more than she can bear:

> *When Rachel saw that she was not bearing Jacob any children, she became jealous of her sister. So she said to Jacob, "Give me children, or I'll die!"* (Gen. 30:1)

"I'll die of shame." Nothing was worse for a woman in that culture than barrenness, not being able to produce children.

Even today, in our culture, there are few pains greater than wanting to have a child, and not being able to. I remember a young husband in the church coming to an Elder meeting, and saying to the other men, "What do you say when every month your wife says to you, 'You should have married somebody else.'" The pain of childlessness. "Give me children, or I'll die!"

Jacob is angry and frustrated:

Jacob became angry with her and said, "Am I in the place of God [not Yahweh, just the deity], *who has kept you from having children?"* (Gen. 30:2)

"What do you want me to do? I'm not the deity. I can't make it happen."

Rachel, in her frustration, settles on a halfway solution. According to her culture, her attendant is her personal property. If her maid can get pregnant and bear a child, that child will belong to Rachel. Kind of like using a surrogate mother and then adopting—the child will be Rachel's.

Then she said, "Here is Bilhah, my servant. Sleep with her so that she can bear children for me and I too can build a family through her." (Gen. 30:3)

The phrase "so that she can bear children for me" in the Hebrew language is literally, "so that she may bear on my knees." The adoptive mother would place her knees, her lap, under the birth canal so that when the baby emerged it would fall into her lap, between her legs, as though she herself had given birth to it. And the baby would be considered hers.

And that's what they did:

So she gave him her servant Bilhah as a wife. Jacob slept with her, and she became pregnant and bore him a son. Then Rachel said, "God [Not Yahweh, the Lord, but the deity] *has vindicated me; he has listened to my plea and given me a son." Because of this she named him Dan.* (Gen. 30:4–6)

Dan means "vindication." "Ah-ha! So there! God has vindicated me."

When Rachel saw that she could provide Jacob sons through this surrogate-adoption procedure, she did it again:

Rachel's servant Bilhah conceived again and bore Jacob a second son. Then Rachel said, "I have had a great struggle with my sister, and I have won." So she named him Naphtali. (Gen. 30:7–8)

Napthali means "an all-out struggle." The Hebrew language repeats the word—"I struggled a great struggle"—to show the intensity of Rachel's determination. She is using every means at her disposal to outdo Leah in giving Jacob children. Leah has stopped bearing, but Rachel is now on a roll. She'll show Leah a thing or two.

The strife and competition and jabbing intensifies, as Leah's attitude becomes one of, "Oh yeah? Well, two can play at that game."

> *When Leah saw that she had stopped having children, she took her servant Zilpah and gave her to Jacob as a wife. Leah's servant Zilpah bore Jacob a son. Then Leah said, "What good fortune!" So she named him Gad.* (Gen. 30:9–11)

Gad means either, "What good fortune," or "A troop is coming." "Get ready for another bunch. Watch me produce now, through my maid."

And sure enough, Leah's maid bears another:

> *Leah's servant Zilpah bore Jacob a second son. Then Leah said, "How happy I am! The women will call me happy." So she named him Asher.* (Gen. 30:12-13)

Asher means "happy." "All right! Look, everybody, how happy I am."

All through this section, the names of the children reflect the strife and competition, the friction and conflict. And sometimes this is our experience too.

We go through periods of strife and conflict in our homes, our marriages, and with our children.

We have seasons of bickering and jealousy with our friends. Things are said that shouldn't have been said, and friendships are strained.

We have misunderstandings and resentments with our parents, with people at work, and with people at church.

We find ourselves frustrated, thinking of angry things to say, ways to get back. And if there's ever a time when we might think God is throwing up his hands, giving up on us, we discover instead that he is wonderfully and lovingly adding more pieces to his good plan.

(More scattered geometric pieces appear on the screen.)

Finally, as we continue, the members of the family begin to move from sorrow and strife to a small obedience. They begin to talk to each other, to hear each other, to come together. They begin to see each other's hurts and needs. And in small, imperfect ways, they move toward peace. Their efforts are feeble and faulty. But God is there, continuing to carry out his good plans.

It begins when Leah's oldest son Reuben—he's five years old—comes home with some beautiful wild plants. Leah immediately recognizes them as mandrake plants—leafy plants that have large yellow berries, about the size of small plums. Mandrake plants were widely viewed as an aid to fertility, sort of a female hormone pill to stimulate fertility.

The small boy Reuben brings them to his mother, Leah. Rachel is there. She sees the mandrakes, and with pleading in her voice says to her sister, "Please, can I have some of the mandrakes? I've never been able to have a child. Please help me."

Leah answers back with her continuing sorrow. "Jacob hasn't slept with me for over a year. You have his heart. And now you want it all—his love *and* the chance to bear his child?"

Rachel also hears the pain of her sister. Leah has stopped bearing children, so Jacob hasn't had any reason to be intimate with her, since he doesn't love her. And so the two sisters take small steps toward peace and obedience—Leah will give Rachel some mandrakes, and Rachel will make sure Jacob sleeps with Leah again. And as a result, both sisters conceive and bear children, and the personal intimate name of Yahweh comes back into the home:

> During wheat harvest, Reuben went out into the fields and found some mandrake plants, which he brought to his mother Leah. Rachel said to Leah, "Please give me some of your son's mandrakes."
>
> But she said to her, "Wasn't it enough that you took away my husband? Will you take my son's mandrakes too?"
>
> "Very well," Rachel said, "he can sleep with you tonight in return for your son's mandrakes."

So when Jacob came in from the fields that evening, Leah went out to meet him. "You must sleep with me," she said. "I have hired you with my son's mandrakes." So he slept with her that night.

God listened to Leah, and she became pregnant and bore Jacob a fifth son. Then Leah said, "God has rewarded me for giving my servant to my husband." So she named him Issachar.

Leah conceived again and bore Jacob a sixth son. Then Leah said, "God has presented me with a precious gift. This time my husband will treat me with honor, because I have borne him six sons." So she named him Zebulun.

Some time later she gave birth to a daughter and named her Dinah.

Then God remembered Rachel; he listened to her and enabled her to conceive. She became pregnant and gave birth to a son and said, "God has taken away my disgrace." She named him Joseph, and said, "May the Lord [Yahweh, my personal intimate God] *add to me another son."* (Gen. 30:14–24)

And now the names of the children reflect the small, halting steps of obedience.

Issachar means "reward." "I bargained with my sister in order to hire you. Tonight you're my reward or wages as a result of our agreement."

Zebulun means "honor." "My honor is returning. Surely my husband will see my value now."

Dinah is the feminine form of Dan—a softer "vindication." "God has established my worth."

Joseph means "may he add." "At last I have borne a child. God has taken away my disgrace. May this not be the last one. May God add another!"

In the next chapter we'll see the two sisters continuing to move toward peace and obedience—working together for the good of the family, cooperating with each other, pulling the family in the same direction, emerging together as the ancestors of the nation Israel.

When we recognize the hurts and sorrows of someone else, when see that perhaps some of our actions have contributed to the strife, when we, even in small ways, reach out in softness and peace, we begin to see glimpses of God's good intentions. And we sense that he is adding even more pieces to his good plan.

(A final set of geometric shapes appears scattered on the screen, along with the former ones.)

Twelve children in seven years. God is making good on his promise to Jacob. Despite the sorrow and strife, with just small, imperfect steps of obedience, God fulfills his good intentions.

The children were everywhere. The promise of God was all over the place—twelve children, all under seven years of age.

They were into everything. One by one they learned to crawl and walk. They learned to talk, after a fashion, and to scream. They learned to poke and pinch and slap and pull hair and throw food. You could always count on one of them to have diarrhea, and two of them to throw up after a meal.

At any given time Jacob could see one boy pounding another boy's head against the floor, three boys trying to shove a fourth into a basket, another biting the head off a pet turtle, another nursing, and Dinah, the little girl, trying to stick her foot in her mouth.

The promise of God was all over the place. They were the dust that would cover the earth. Kicking, howling, screaming, slobbering, spitting, and fighting—they were God's great promise and the earth's great blessing.

There were times when Jacob would look at them and think—You're so noisy . . . so messy . . . so important. And he knew God that was good to him.

My friend, as your life moves through times of sorrow and strife and small obedience, God is adding the pieces of his plan. Though you may not see it, the promise of God is all over the place. And little by little . . . *(three of the scattered pieces come together on the screen)* God is bringing together . . . *(two more pieces are joined to the emerging image)* his good plan for your life *(the final three pieces complete the six-pointed star).*

11

STREAKED, SPECKLED, AND SPOTTED

Genesis 30:25–43

(Walk around the platform and aisles clapping hands.)
"What are you doing?" "I'm keeping the alligators away." "There are no alligators around here." "Works, doesn't it!"

If you clap your hands to get success, and success comes, is it because you clapped your hands?

If you carry a rabbit's foot, and have good luck that day, is it because you were carrying a rabbit's foot?

When I was on the baseball team in high school, one game I went three for four, including a home run and a triple. For lunch that day before the game, I had a cheese sandwich. The next game, if I ate a cheese sandwich for lunch again, and again went three for four, would it be because of the cheese sandwich?

If you color your hair to attract a boy, or you lift weights to attract a girl, and then you attract someone, is it because you colored your hair or lifted weights?

If you study hard and get a college degree in order to find good employment, when you graduate and find good employment, is it because you studied hard and got the degree?

If you work well on the job, put in extra time, and make money for the company, in order to get a better job with a bigger company—if you do these things in order to get success, and success comes, is it because you did these things?

(Clap hands) If you clap your hands, and no alligators come, is it because you clapped your hands?

There was a time when Jacob thought so—he thought that success came because he did certain things. But he learned differently. He learned that when you do certain things to get success, and success comes, it's *not* because you did those things, it's because of something else.

Success comes not because of what you do, but because of something else.

It all began when he turned in his resignation to his father-in-law, Laban. He wanted to leave and start his own business. For the past fourteen years he'd been working for Laban, and he'd made Laban rich. But Jacob himself had nothing to show for those fourteen years. He'd been working for free—that was the bride price required for him to marry Laban's two daughters. Now he wanted to return to his own country. But he had nothing—no wealth or assets or capital to go back and start his own business.

So he turns in his resignation to his father-in-law. He tells him he wants to return to his own country, and suggests to him the idea of a going-away party, with a gold watch, or better yet, a golden parachute. He asks Laban to send him off with some large bonus in appreciation for all Jacob has done for him. This bonus would become the venture capital he needs to start up business in his own country.

But Laban refuses to give Jacob anything to send him on his way. We'll see why in a minute. So Jacob comes up with another plan, a course of action he believes will enable him to achieve his goals. He says to himself, "Since Laban won't give me any start-up capital, then here's what I'm going to do to get the wealth and success I want."

And sure enough, when Jacob puts his plan into action, the wealth and success come. And Jacob assumes it's because of the things he did. But he later learns that's not the case. The success came not because of what he did, but because of something else.

What is that something else? If success is not because of what we do, then why is it? What does cause our success? The answer begins to emerge as Jacob turns in his resignation, and asks his father-in-law for a going-away gift to start a business in his own land.

After Rachel gave birth to Joseph, Jacob said to Laban, "Send me on my way so I can go back to my own homeland. Give me my wives and children, for whom I have served you, and I will be on my way. You know how much work I've done for you." (Gen. 30:25–26)

When Jacob says, "Send me on my way," he's saying, "Give me my wives' share of the family inheritance. Send us off with whatever would be their share of the family estate." This is an appropriate request, given the customs of the day, and even more so given the fourteen years of free labor Jacob has given Laban. "I want to leave. Send me off with a reasonable amount of money, either due to my wives or in recognition for how much good I've done for you."

But Laban, tight-fisted and shrewd, smiles very politely and says, "No, that's not going to happen. I don't owe you anything, and I want you to stay."

But Laban said to him, "If I have found favor in your eyes, please stay. I have learned by divination that the LORD has blessed me because of you." He added, "Name your wages, and I will pay them." (Gen. 30:27–28)

"Surely, Jacob, these have been good years for you. We're one big happy family here. Why would you want to leave? You don't need to go. Stay."

And then Laban adds, "Besides that, I don't really owe you any back pay. Were there some wages we agreed on that I haven't paid you? No, our contract was that you would work for free for my two daughters. If you're under some different impression, name what I owe you and I'll give it to you."

Laban doesn't want Jacob to leave. He isn't going to give him anything to make it possible. Laban has learned over the fourteen years that having Jacob working for him is the best thing that ever happened to him. For some reason, ever since Jacob came, Laban's assets and net worth have gone up every year. And Laban has come to the conclusion it's because of Jacob: "I have learned by divination that the LORD has blessed me because of you." Meaning, "Jacob, I've gone to fortune tellers, I've consulted tarot cards, I've read tea leaves, I've rolled bones—I've tried every means I know to find out why so much good fortune and blessing has come over these past years, and every time the answer comes back the same—it's you, Jacob! For some reason, the Lord has blessed me because of you, and I don't want you to leave. So I'm not going to make it easy for you to go."

Jacob appeals again. "Yes, it's true—everything I've touched for you has turned to gold. Surely there ought to be some reward for me. I have my own family now to consider."

> Jacob said to him, "You know how I have worked for you and how your livestock has fared under my care. The little you had before I came has increased greatly, and the Lord has blessed you wherever I have been. But now, when may I do something for my own household?" (Gen. 30:29–30)

"Laban, I took you from a small mom-and-pop outfit to a fifty-million-dollar operation. Whatever I gave my attention to—your flocks, your farmlands, your tents, your spinning wheels, your weaving looms—wherever I went, the Lord blessed you. But now it's time for me to think of how I'm going to support my own family."

The two men are at a standstill. Jacob needs start-up funds to return to his own country. But Laban won't give him any money. On the other hand, Laban knows that Jacob won't stay and continue working for free now that the fourteen-year contract is over. But he doesn't want to lose Jacob because of all the benefit Jacob brings him.

To solve the dilemma, Laban proposes that they enter into a new contract—one that will eventually provide Jacob the money he wants, but one that will still keep him around so that Laban can continue to benefit from him. "What shall I give you?" he asked (30:31). What salary will it take to keep you here? Let's have a new agreement on what your wages will be.

Jacob's answer is, "If that's the way it has to be, then rather than a salary, I want a percentage of the profits. I want a profit-sharing contract—one that says that any new animal born to your flocks and herds that has a certain coloring or marking will be mine, and all the rest will be yours.

Here's what Jacob has in mind: Almost universally, all sheep are white, and all goats are black or brown. That's the normal coloring for the flocks of the day—all the animals are solid colors. The sheep are born solid white, and the goats are born solid dark—brown or black.

But there's a recessive gene that occasionally shows up, and when it does, an animal will be born with an odd coloring or marking. Because the gene is recessive, such births are rare, but Jacob proposes that when they do occur, these animals will be his. Specifically, any sheep that is born speckled or dark, instead of solid white, will be his. And any goat that's born with white spots or streaks, instead of solid dark, will also be his. In other words, any animal that isn't a solid color—solid white sheep or solid dark goat— any animal that's born streaked, speckled, or spotted will be his wages.

Jacob proposes to start this new agreement by separating or removing out of Laban's flocks whatever animals are currently showing this recessive gene. He'll start with whatever few odd-colored animals are currently in the flocks, and then keep any young they breed that continue to show the recessive gene. But if they breed a solid-colored animal, that will go back into Laban's flock. At the same time, if any of Laban's solid-colored animals happen to breed an odd-colored animal, that will be Jacob's.

Laban can inspect Jacob's flock whenever he wants. If he finds any solid-colored animal in it, he can accuse Jacob of stealing, for the agreement is that Jacob only gets the odd-colored ones.

While Jacob will continue to manage Laban's flocks, he'll start his own flock through this arrangement:

> "What shall I give you?" he asked.
>
> "Don't give me anything," Jacob replied. "But if you will do this one thing for me, I will go on tending your flocks and watching over them: Let me go through all your flocks today and remove from them every speckled or spotted sheep, every dark-colored lamb and every spotted or speckled goat. They will be my wages. And my honesty will testify for me in the future, whenever you check on the wages you have paid me. Any goat in my possession that is not speckled or spotted, or any lamb that is not dark-colored, will be considered stolen." (Gen. 30:31–33)

Laban can't agree fast enough to this proposal. "Done, Jacob! Let's sign it, just as you've said!" Laban can't believe this new arrangement. At best he figures Jacob's only going to get one to two percent of new births, because that's about how often the recessive gene shows up. And ordinarily, in their culture, profit-sharing agreements are figured at twenty percent of all new births, not one to two percent. Laban can't believe his good fortune—it'll take Jacob years to build up a flock big enough for him to leave. And in the meantime, Laban will continue to grow richer and richer.

And just to make sure that Jacob gets off to a poor start, Laban tells his sons to go through his flocks before Jacob has a chance to and remove out all the odd-colored ones and pack them off three days' distance, leaving Jacob to find nothing but solid animals in Laban's flocks to begin with.

> *"Agreed," said Laban. "Let it be as you have said." That same day he removed all the male goats that were streaked or spotted, and all the speckled or spotted female goats* (all that had white on them) and all the dark-colored lambs, and he placed them in the care of his sons. Then he put a three-day journey between himself and Jacob, while Jacob continued to tend the rest of Laban's flocks. (Gen. 30:34–36)

Laban's dishonesty has put Jacob at a disadvantage. Jacob now, apparently, has no animals with recessive genes in the flock that Laban has left him to work with. But Jacob has a plan. And Jacob begins to do some things that he thinks will bring him the wealth and success he wants. And sure enough, when Jacob does those things, when he puts his plan into operation, the wealth, the success comes. And Jacob assumes that it's because of the things he did. But that's not the case. The success is not because of what he did, but because of something else.

Here's his plan. He says himself, "I'm starting with nothing but solids— all white sheep and all dark goats. How can I breed odd-colored animals from them? How can I get white sheep to give birth to dark sheep, and how can I get dark goats to give birth to white-splotched goats? And how can I make sure that these odd-colored young are strong and healthy enough so that they can keep on breeding and multiplying their recessive colors?"

And he comes up with a plan for the goats and a plan for the sheep.

Here's his plan to get Laban's dark goats to breed white-splotched goats. He cuts branches from trees that have a white wood. He peels strips of the dark bark from the branches, so that rings of the white wood show up through the dark branch. Then he places these white-streaked branches in the watering troughs. As the goats are drinking and then mating, while looking at these streaked branches, the result will be that these dark goats give birth to white-streaked goats instead of dark ones. And these white-streaked goats will become Jacob's.

How to get Laban's white sheep to breed dark sheep? He arranges the white sheep so that they will mate while they are looking at some dark or splotched animal—any animal with color—either one of Laban's dark goats or one of Jacob's own splotched animals. As these white sheep mate while looking at dark or splotched animals, the result will be that these solid white sheep then give birth to dark or splotched sheep. And these odd-colored sheep will become Jacob's.

For both goats and sheep, he's only going to keep the strongest, healthiest animals to breed his own flocks. If he sees a weak or sickly animal, regardless of what color it is, he'll leave it in Laban's flocks—any animal it breeds would probably be stillborn. Jacob's only going to work with strong animals.

That's his plan:

> Jacob, however, took fresh-cut branches from poplar, almond and plane trees and made white stripes on them by peeling the bark and exposing the white inner wood of the branches. Then he placed the peeled branches in all the watering troughs, so that they would be directly in front of the flocks when they came to drink. When the flocks were in heat and came to drink, they mated in front of the branches. And they [the dark goats] bore young that were streaked or speckled or spotted. Jacob set apart the young [spotted goats] of the flock by themselves, but made the rest [the white sheep] face the streaked and dark-colored animals that belonged to Laban. Thus he made separate flocks for himself and did not put them with Laban's animals. Whenever the stronger females were in heat, Jacob would place the branches in the troughs in front of the animals so they would mate near the branches, but if the animals were weak, he would not place them there. So the weak animals went to Laban and the strong ones to Jacob. (Gen. 30:37–42)

Over the next six years (cf. Gen. 31:38–42), using this plan, Jacob gets all of Laban's solid dark goats to breed white-splotched animals, and all of Laban's solid white sheep to breed either dark sheep or at least sheep with dark splotchy markings. These animals all become Jacob's flock, and then they continue to pass down their recessive gene.

At the end of six years, Laban's flock of solid white sheep and solid dark goats has dwindled to almost nothing, while Jacob's speckled and splotched herds have filled the land. Jacob has to hire many servants to care for his vast holdings, and he has to invest in countless pack animals—camels and donkeys—to transport his wool and meat to markets throughout the area. Jacob is rich.

In this way the man grew exceedingly prosperous and came to own large flocks, and female and male servants, and camels and donkeys. (Gen. 30:43)

Jacob put his plans and schemes to work to get the wealth he wanted. "I will do these things," he said, "to get success. I will mate Laban's solid dark goats while they are looking at white-peeled branches, and I will mate his solid white sheep while they looking at dark or splotched animals, and thus I will breed the pattern I want." He does these things, and success comes. But when success comes, is it because he did these things? Is it his plan, his scheme, his work, that brought him success?

We read about what he does, and we say, "I may not know much about animals or breeding, but I'm pretty sure it doesn't work this way—that what the animals look at while mating will leave a mark on the fetus." This sounds like the tabloid headlines we sometimes see while shopping at the grocery store—"Pregnant mother frightened by wolf, gives birth to baby with fangs!" And we say, "I don't think so."

Is it because of what Jacob's animals were looking at while they mated that he got his vast splotched herds? If I clap my hands and no alligators come, is it because I clapped my hands? Jacob did these things because he thought they would bring him success. And success came. But was it because he did these things?

The answer is no. And Jacob himself soon came to realize it. He soon came to realize that the reason success came was not because of his plans and schemes, but because of God's love. His success was not because of his skills or cleverness, but because God had committed to bless him. It was not because of anything he did, but only because God had promised him good.

It was sometime toward the end of his six years of breeding that Jacob realized this. At the time he was still taking Laban's solid-colored animals and exposing them to peeled branches or splotched animals, thinking this was what was bringing him success. But God came to Jacob in a dream. And God said to him, "Jacob, it's not your plan that's bringing you success. You think you've found a clever way to make all of Laban's solid animals produce odd-colored ones. That's not the case, Jacob. It's not you, it's me."

In the dream, God has Jacob look at Laban's animals that he's using. "Jacob, notice that Laban's animals are not really solid. Notice that all of these dream animals, even before they mate, are already showing the recessive gene—they're all splotched or speckled. The dream tells you, Jacob, that it's actually me inside of all of Laban's animals, altering their genetic code, controlling their hereditary traits. It's not your having them look at streaked branches or other animals. It's me, Jacob, controlling their birthing patterns. Your success, Jacob, is not because of what you have done, but because I have determined to bless you."

Somewhere toward the end of his six years of breeding, Jacob learned all this in a dream. We read it in the next chapter, as he explains this to his wives.

> "In breeding season I once had a dream in which I looked up and saw that the male goats mating with the flock were [already] streaked, speckled or spotted. The angel of God said to me in the dream, 'Jacob.' I answered, 'Here I am.' And he said, 'Look up and see that all the male goats mating with the flock are streaked, speckled or spotted, for I have seen all that Laban has been doing to you. I am the God of Bethel, where you anointed a pillar and where you made a vow to me.'" (Gen. 31:10–13a)

God says, "I see how Laban is trying to take advantage of you and keep you near him, but I'm the God who promised you blessing back at Bethel, and I'm controlling the reproduction of the flocks to make it possible for you to return."

My friend, if success comes, it's not because of your skills, but because of God's love. If good things have happened in your life, it's not because of how smart you are or how hard you've worked, but only because God has determined to bless you.

Are you educated? It's not because of your brain. It's because God gave you a family and a support system, and time and money to let it happen.

Have you married well? It's not because you're so attractive and winsome and desirable. It's because God has chosen this gift of a spouse for you.

Are you doing well in your job? It's not because of your skills and your clever work. It's because God has determined that through Christ Jesus, he will bring good things to your life.

Whatever has come to us, it is the Lord's goodness that has brought it to us.

12

AGAINST ALL ODDS AND GODS

Genesis 31

The Scripture we're going to look at speaks to those who are at different stages along a path.

Some of you are at the start of the path. In your heart you feel that God has good plans for you. As you've come to know him, you sense that he intends to do you good. As he starts down the path with you, he promises good things ahead—education, degrees, career, marriage, family, a new position in your company, maybe owning your own business. Somewhere, ahead of you, are the good promises of God.

Your question as you start on the path is: Will God provide what he's promised? Will it come true? Will he do what he says? To you, the message from God's Word is: What God promises, he provides. What he intends, he gives.

Others of you are farther along the path. You're at the stage where, yes, God has provided. He's been good. He's done what he said he would do. He's provided degrees and a job. You're in the midst of raising a family. You've moved into a home and you're settling in. He's provided, but now it's being threatened. It's under attack. His provision is vulnerable. There's some question whether it will remain. Your company is downsizing, or you have a new boss and for some reason you're not in favor with him. Or there's tension in the family—friction, hardness, lack of communication. Maybe your business or career seems stalled, your income potentially jeopardized.

Things are still okay, but your question is: Will the provision continue? Will it stay? Or will it be lost? And to you, the message from God's Word is: What God provides, he protects. What he gives, he guards.

This is the message for all of us—What God promises, he provides, and what he provides, he protects. This is what Jacob learned—What God promises, he provides, and what he gives, he guards.

Let's first bring together the promises Jacob had, so that we can see that what God promised, he provided. Then, when this provision was threatened, when it was under attack, when it looked like someone would take it away, let's see that what God provided, he protected.

The promises Jacob had are that God would bless him, that his descendants would be as thick as the dust of the earth, that he would be rich and his line would extend to all points of the compass, and that he would be a blessing to others.

Let's briefly pull together these promises.

The promises started even before Jacob was born—the promise that he would be chosen and favored over his older brother, and would become a nation of people. This is what God told his mother during her pregnancy:

> The Lord said to her,
> "Two nations are in your womb,
>   and two peoples from within you will be separated;
>   one people will be stronger than the other,
>   and the older will serve the younger." (Gen. 25:23)

There's the promise that he, the younger, would be chosen and favored, and would become a great nation.

When it came time for him to receive the family blessing, his father repeated God's promises to him—that he would become rich, favored over others, and a source of blessing to many:

> May God give you heaven's dew
>   and earth's richness—
>   an abundance of grain and new wine.
> May nations serve you
>   and peoples bow down to you.
> Be lord over your brothers,
>   and may the sons of your mother bow down to you.

> *May those who curse you be cursed*
> *and those who bless you be blessed.* (Gen. 27:28–29)

Promises of riches, favor, and blessing.

He was forced to flee his homeland to escape the anger of his brother. But before he left, his father blessed him, again confirming God's promises to him:

> *"May God Almighty bless you and make you fruitful and increase your numbers until you become a community of peoples. May he give you and your descendants the blessing given to Abraham."* (Gen. 28:3–4a)

He fled his family and his country in haste. Would God's promises go with him to a strange land? Yes. The last night, before he crossed the border, God came to him in a dream and again repeated the promises:

> *"I am the Lord, the God of your father Abraham and the God of Isaac. I will give you and your descendants the land on which you are lying. Your descendants will be like the dust of the earth, and you will spread out to the west and to the east, to the north and to the south. All peoples on earth will be blessed through you and your offspring. I am with you and will watch over you wherever you go, and I will bring you back to this land. I will not leave you until I have done what I have promised you.* (Gen. 28:13b–15)

These are the promises—that he would marry, that his descendants would be as thick as the dust of the earth, that he would be rich and spread to all points of the compass, that he would be a blessing to others, and that God would be with him and never leave him until he'd done everything he said.

And what God promised, he provided. What God said he would do, he did.

Jacob traveled five hundred miles to a strange land, and met a girl. In fourteen years, through a strange mixture of ancient customs and in-law treachery, he ended up with two wives, two maids, and eleven sons and one daughter, from whom would come the descendants that would be as thick as the dust of the earth.

Along the way he blessed his father-in-law—he made him rich. But his father-in-law was ungrateful for the blessing, and attempted to take advantage of him. His father-in-law cheated him at every opportunity, and changed his salary downward ten times. But over the next six years, God fulfilled his promise to make Jacob rich, and he began to spread out with herds and flocks and servants, and pack animals to transport his products to markets in all directions:

> *The man grew exceedingly prosperous and came to own large flocks, and female and male servants, and camels and donkeys.* (Gen. 30:43)

What God promised, he provided. It didn't always happen the way Jacob thought it would happen—his domestic affairs were certainly not what he expected. There were times of friction and irritation between his wives. The children probably came faster and messier than he was prepared for. The time frame for all this may have been different than what he thought it would be—it took twenty years. But in the end, God had done exactly what he said he would do—Jacob was married, with innumerable children, rich beyond expectation, and a source of blessing to many.

And to those of you who are starting down the same path, to you the message from God's Word is this—what God promises he provides. It may not happen the way you think. Or in the time you expect. There may be times along the way when life will get messy. But the truth is absolutely certain—what God promises, he provides.

But then, all of a sudden, things change for Jacob. And he finds himself at the stage that others of you are at. God's provision is threatened. It comes under attack. There's some question whether it will remain. Will God protect what he's provided?

Laban and his sons turn against Jacob. Jacob's wealth has come at their expense. Laban tried to take advantage of Jacob, and cheated him at every opportunity. But God instead transferred all of Laban's wealth to Jacob.

Laban and his sons now begin to have dark thoughts against Jacob. Jacob's still the newcomer in their midst. Though he's married into their family, their loyalties are still to one another and the family business. And Jacob suddenly perceives that he's become *persona non grata*, and that they might take everything from him. And that's how our passage opens—Jacob notices that Laban and his sons have turned against him. They're resentful of his wealth and threatening to seize it from him:

> Jacob heard that Laban's sons were saying, "Jacob has taken everything our father owned and has gained all this wealth from what belonged to our father." And Jacob noticed that Laban's attitude toward him was not what it had been. (Gen. 31:1–2)

Jacob is vulnerable. If he stays, he could lose everything. But it he goes back to his own land, his brother could kill him. What should he do? Everything is threatened, under attack. Will God's provision continue, or will it be lost?

The rest of the chapter shows that the truth is absolutely certain—what God provides, he protects. What he gives, he guards.

As Jacob ponders what to do, God comes to him and says, "Jacob, return to your own land. And I will protect you."

> Then the Lord said to Jacob, "Go back to the land of your fathers and to your relatives, and I will be with you." (Gen. 31:3)

"I will be with you." There it is again—the language of the promise. It's been twenty years since Jacob has heard from God, twenty years since he fled his homeland. And in those twenty years, God has provided all he promised. And now, at the end of the twenty years, God's closing words repeat the earlier promise: "I will be with you." "I will guard what I have given you. What I've provided, I will protect." He's to return to his own land, and God will protect him from Esau.

Jacob asks his wives to meet him out in the pasture lands, where their words won't be overheard by others. He wants to know if his wives will go with him. They were born and raised in this land. They have small children, who have only known this country. But God has blessed him, and told him to return to his own land. Will they go with him? Are their loyalties with him or their father?

> So Jacob sent word to Rachel and Leah to come out to the fields where his flocks were. He said to them, "I see that your father's attitude

toward me is not what it was before, but the God of my father has been with me. You know that I've worked for your father with all my strength, yet your father has cheated me by changing my wages ten times. However, God has not allowed him to harm me. If he said, 'The speckled ones will be your wages,' then all the flocks gave birth to speckled young; and if he said, 'The streaked ones will be your wages,' then all the flocks bore streaked young. So God has taken away your father's livestock and has given them to me.

"In breeding season I once had a dream in which I looked up and saw that the male goats mating with the flock were streaked, speckled or spotted. The angel of God said to me in the dream, 'Jacob.' I answered, 'Here I am.' And he said, 'Look up and see that all the male goats mating with the flock are streaked, speckled or spotted, for I have seen all that Laban has been doing to you. I am the God of Bethel, where you anointed a pillar and where you made a vow to me. Now leave this land at once and go back to your native land.'" (Gen. 31:4–13)

Their answer is, "We'll go with you." They've seen their father turn sour over the years. They've seen him try to take advantage of Jacob at every opportunity. There's nothing left of their father's estate for them. They have no reason to stay. Their loyalties are now with Jacob. Their response is, "Do what God is telling you to do."

Then Rachel and Leah replied, "Do we still have any share in the inheritance of our father's estate? Does he not regard us as foreigners? Not only has he sold us, but he has used up what was paid for us. Surely all the wealth that God took away from our father belongs to us and our children. So do whatever God has told you." (Gen. 31:14–16)

Jacob makes the decision to leave, but as is so often the case, he goes about it the wrong way. He sneaks off while Laban and his sons are away, occupied for several days at a distant sheep-shearing site. Jacob leaves without telling Laban that he's going. He's afraid if he lets Laban know, Laban will take action against him and prevent him from leaving. Jacob doesn't yet fully trust that what God provided, God will protect.

Then Jacob put his children and his wives on camels, and he drove all his livestock ahead of him, along with all the goods he had accumulated in Paddan Aram, to go to his father Isaac in the land of Canaan.

When Laban had gone to shear his sheep, Rachel stole her father's household gods. Moreover, Jacob deceived Laban the Aramean by not telling him he was running away. So he fled with all he had, crossed the Euphrates River, and headed for the hill country of Gilead. (Gen. 31:17–21)

Jacob leaves without notice. This is the wrong way to go about it. It's discourteous. It's disrespectful. It doesn't give Laban a chance to say goodbye to his daughters and grandchildren.

But Laban will have even greater problems with what Jacob has done. What's more serious to Laban than Jacob's disrespect is that someone has stolen his household gods. These household gods were small images that were passed down from generation to generation. They were the center of family worship. They were viewed as the spiritual force responsible for the family's prosperity. In each generation, these household images would be passed on to the eldest in the family, and would continue to be honored and worshipped as the source of the family's ongoing fortunes.

Rachel takes these gods, to rub salt in the family's reliance on them and to show that they are essentially impotent. These gods couldn't protect Laban's prosperity. They brought no fortune to Laban's family. The family she's leaving is impoverished. All the family's wealth has gone over to Jacob. Jacob's God is stronger. Rachel steals Laban's gods to show him that they are useless to him.

When Laban discovers that Jacob and his daughters and his grandchildren, and Jacob's entire operation, have secretly left, and that his gods are gone, he sets out after him. He's going to accuse Jacob of disrespect. But mostly he wants his household gods back.

He catches up with Jacob, and spits out his anger and accusations against him. "Why did you sneak off? I would have thrown you a going-away party. You didn't even give me a chance to kiss my daughters and grandchildren goodbye. You've acted foolishly. But also you've acted wrongly—you've stolen my gods, and I want them back."

> On the third day Laban was told that Jacob had fled. Taking his relatives with him, he pursued Jacob for seven days and caught up with him in the hill country of Gilead. Then God came to Laban the Aramean in a dream at night and said to him, "Be careful not to say anything to Jacob, either good or bad."
>
> Jacob had pitched his tent in the hill country of Gilead when Laban overtook him, and Laban and his relatives camped there too. Then Laban said to Jacob, "What have you done? You've deceived me, and you've carried off my daughters like captives in war. Why did you run off secretly and deceive me? Why didn't you tell me, so I could send you away with joy and singing to the music of timbrels and harps? You didn't even let me kiss my grandchildren and my daughters goodbye. You have done a foolish thing. I have the power to harm you; but last night the God of your father said to me, 'Be careful not to say anything to Jacob, either good or bad.' Now you have gone off because you longed to return to your father's household. But why did you steal my gods?" (Gen. 31:22–30)

And as Laban accuses Jacob of having stolen his gods, the confrontation now becomes a battle of the gods—Laban's gods against Jacob's God. Can Laban's gods assert themselves? Can Laban's gods reveal themselves among Jacob's stuff? Can Laban's gods bring his daughters and grandchildren back home with him? Can Laban's gods punish Jacob, and deprive him of what he has? Can Laban's gods restore Laban's fortune back to him and his sons? Can Laban gods and their blessings be passed on again, from generation to generation, in Laban's family?

As the confrontation becomes a battle of the gods, the question of "protecting what has been provided" now moves to a larger dimension. The question now is not simply whether God can protect Jacob from an angry father-in-law, from a greedy manipulative employer who has continually tried to cheat him. The question now is: Can God protect Jacob from these gods, from these hostile spiritual powers? Can God protect him from the evil force behind these gods, from the demonic powers they represent?

He's provided for Jacob against all odds. But can he now protect what he's provided against all gods?

And that's really the question for us—Can God protect us from Satan's desire to harm us? For that's ultimately who our enemy is. Behind any human opposition, behind any economic tragedy, behind any threat or attack, behind any attempt to take God's blessing from us, ultimately behind it all is the evil power of our enemy Satan. And the question is: Can God protect what he's provided?

And so Laban's confrontation sets up the question: Whose god will be more powerful—Laban's or Jacob's? Laban's gods have gotten off to a poor start. They couldn't prevent themselves from being carted off. They couldn't prevent themselves from being stolen. They've lost round one in the battle. But Laban is going to give them a chance to reassert themselves, to reveal themselves among Jacob's stuff. Laban's going to give them a chance to act again on his behalf. Can God protect what he's provided?

Jacob is stung by Laban's two charges—that his leaving was discourteous and disrespectful, and that he's stolen Laban's gods. He explains why he left secretly, but he denies stealing the household gods, since he doesn't know Rachel took them.

> Jacob answered Laban, "I was afraid, because I thought you would take your daughters away from me by force. But if you find anyone who has your gods, that person shall not live. In the presence of our relatives, see for yourself whether there is anything of yours here with me; and if so, take it." Now Jacob did not know that Rachel had stolen the gods. (Gen. 31:31–32)

Laban will now search to recover his gods. And with their power and help, he will restore his fortune, and secure the future for himself and his sons.

But he can't find his gods. They don't reveal themselves, they don't assert themselves. On the contrary, Laban's gods are mocked, they're insulted. Not only are they shown to be impotent, they're actually made fun of, humiliated, the butt of a joke. The purpose in all of this is to show us how ultimately powerless Satan is when God intends to bless us.

The humiliation of the gods is that a woman is supposedly menstruating on them.

So Laban went into Jacob's tent and into Leah's tent and into the tent
of the two female servants, but he found nothing. After he came out of
Leah's tent, he entered Rachel's tent. Now Rachel had taken the house-
hold gods and put them inside her camel's saddle and was sitting on
them. Laban searched through everything in the tent but found nothing.
Rachel said to her father, "Don't be angry, my lord, that I cannot stand
up in your presence; I'm having my period." So he searched but could
not find the household gods. (Gen. 31:33–35)

In their culture, a woman's menstrual period was a time of ceremonial
uncleanness. She wouldn't come into the sanctuary until her period was
over and she had gone through a ritual cleansing ceremony. And in the
meantime, anything that came in contact with her menstrual clothing was
considered soiled.

Rachel sits on her father's gods, deliberately contaminating them, dar-
ing them to have any power to do something about the humiliation she
is causing them. She's showing as much contempt for them as possible—
they're impotent, useless, nothing. Her husband's God is the only real God,
the only one with power. And he will protect what he's provided for them.

Laban searches, but he cannot find his gods. They cannot reveal themselves. After the fruitless search, Jacob sees that Laban is defeated, empty,
bewildered—eyes casting about, wondering what to do next. Jacob now
knows that his God is protecting him against Laban, and so he goes on the
attack. Laban came at him with accusations, but now Jacob hurls accusations back at Laban.

"You didn't find anything, did you? All your accusations, and no evidence to back them up. Laban, I worked for you twenty years, with no appreciation at all. I gave you more effort than any man ever expected or deserved. But you took advantage of me at every opportunity. You took every
nickel and dime from me that you could. Every time it looked like I might
be getting ahead, you arbitrarily changed my wages downward. Ten times!
But my God has been with me, providing what he promised, and now protecting me from you."

Jacob goes on the attack, and hurls accusations back at Laban.

Jacob was angry and took Laban to task. "What is my crime?" he asked Laban. "How have I wronged you that you hunt me down? Now that you have searched through all my goods, what have you found that belongs to your household? Put it here in front of your relatives and mine, and let them judge between the two of us.

"I have been with you for twenty years now. Your sheep and goats have not miscarried, nor have I eaten rams from your flocks. I did not bring you animals torn by wild beasts; I bore the loss myself. And you demanded payment from me for whatever was stolen by day or night. This was my situation: The heat consumed me in the daytime and the cold at night, and sleep fled from my eyes. It was like this for the twenty years I was in your household. I worked for you fourteen years for your two daughters and six years for your flocks, and you changed my wages ten times. If the God of my father, the God of Abraham and the Fear of Isaac, had not been with me, you would surely have sent me away empty-handed. But God has seen my hardship and the toil of my hands, and last night he rebuked you." (Gen. 31:36–42)

"You and your gods have attempted to keep me down, but my God—the God of Abraham, and the Fear of Isaac—the one before whom you ought to stand in fear and awe and terror—my God has provided and protected."

Laban is defeated, empty. He's reduced to pitiful pleading. "Jacob, you've got everything—my daughters, my grandchildren, my wealth. And there's nothing I can do about it."

Laban answered Jacob, "The women are my daughters, the children are my children, and the flocks are my flocks. All you see is mine. Yet what can I do today about these daughters of mine, or about the children they have borne? (Gen. 31:43)

Laban is whipped. Jacob's God has provided for Jacob against all odds, and now he has protected him against all gods.

And Laban suddenly realizes that now he's the one who needs protection—protection from Jacob and from Jacob's God. He realizes that God's blessing is going to continually remain on Jacob, and he'll only become stronger and stronger as the years go on. And Laban is afraid that Jacob, in his anger and with the power of his God, might someday decide to return and take revenge against him and his sons. And so he begs Jacob to promise that he won't do him any harm in the future.

"Come now, let's make a covenant, you and I, and let it serve as a witness between us." (Gen. 31:44)

He wants a peace treaty, a covenant, a promise from Jacob that Jacob will treat his daughters well, and that in the future Jacob won't come back to harm him. They set up a memorial marker of stones to signify a border boundary between them, and Laban makes Jacob swear that he won't come across it in the future to take revenge against him. Laban specifies all the language of the treaty, making every effort to protect himself in the future. Jacob lets Laban write it any way he wants. He knows now that he doesn't need this agreement or treaty to protect himself. He knows that his God will protect him. But since he has no intention of ever coming this way again, he agrees to the covenant, and they seal the treaty with a meal.

So Jacob took a stone and set it up as a pillar. He said to his relatives, "Gather some stones." So they took stones and piled them in a heap, and they ate there by the heap. Laban called it Jegar Sahadutha [in Aramaic, "witness heap"], and Jacob called it Galeed [which means the same thing in Hebrew].

Laban said, "This heap is a witness between you and me today." That is why it was called Galeed. It was also called Mizpah ["watchtower, guard tower, military post,"] because he said, "May the Lord keep watch between you and me when we are away from each other. If you mistreat my daughters or if you take any wives besides my daughters, even though no one is with us, remember that God is a witness between you and me." Laban also said to Jacob, "Here is this heap, and here is this pillar I have set up between you and me. This heap is a witness, and this pillar is a witness, that I will not go past this heap to your side to harm you and that you will not go past this heap and pillar to my side to harm me. May the God of Abraham and the God of Nahor, the God of their father, judge between us."

So Jacob took an oath in the name of the Fear of his father Isaac. He offered a sacrifice there in the hill country and invited his relatives to a meal. After they had eaten, they spent the night there.

Early the next morning Laban kissed his grandchildren and his daughters and blessed them. Then he left and returned home. (Gen. 31:45–55)

Laban has the opportunity to say goodbye. But he leaves empty-handed. The wealth . . . the blessing . . . the provision . . . and the power of God—that stays with Jacob.

And so it is with you, my friend. What God intends for you, he will give you. And what he gives, he will guard.

What God promises, he provides. And what he provides, he protects.

And no power is greater than his.

13

TWO CAMPS, TWO CAMPS, TWO CAMPS

Genesis 32:1–21

When our daughter Sarah was in college, she would be asked out on a date by some nice fellow, and the conversation would often start out with the fellow saying to Sarah, "Would you like to get a cup of coffee and some dessert?"

Now, Sarah doesn't drink coffee. And she pretty much doesn't like any kind of dessert—not ice cream, not pie, not cake, not cookies or brownies. But here's this nice fellow asking her out for coffee and dessert. What does she say to him? She wants to go out with him, but does she have to grit her teeth, forcing down the coffee and pretending she likes the dessert? Or can she tell the truth, "I don't like coffee or dessert, but I don't mind watching while you eat." Can she tell the truth, and trust God that the fellow will still want to take her out? Or will her honesty kind of kibosh the relationship from the start?

Somehow they usually get past the awkwardness of this conversation, and the nice fellow soon discovers that Sarah loves potatoes. Any kind of potatoes—baked, mashed, French fried, scalloped, oven roasted. And he soon figures out that a big hit with Sarah is to take her to McDonald's and get her a double order of jumbo fries.

But early on the question is, "Do I have to pretend or compromise to make something happen, or can I be open and honest and trust God to take care of me?"

Now admittedly, for a first date, that's a fairly inconsequential matter. But what if the courtship goes further than that? What if it gets to the point of considering if this is the person I want to marry? Then the question becomes more significant. Should I tell this person that I'm seriously interested in and maybe hope to marry—should I tell him about my health issues, or my financial problems, or my legal difficulties, or my family troubles, or my past sexual history? If I tell him, will it end the relationship, and will I lose something I want very badly—maybe the chance to marry him? Should I protect myself and take matters into my own hands, or can I be straightforward and trust God in the matter?

If I'm applying for a job, can I put out a truthful résumé and trust God to take care of me? Or do I need to disguise the reason I left my last job, and list skills and accomplishments that aren't exactly accurate, to impress the interviewer? Do I need to take matters into my own hands to protect myself, or can I trust God to take care of me?

In the later years of life, when it looks like my spouse or one of my parents will need expensive long-term care, can I be forthright with the social agencies about our financial condition, and trust God to provide? Or do I need to hide income and assets so that government or county services will take over the costs? Do I need to protect myself, or can I trust God in the matter?

That's the question Jacob is struggling with as he makes the long journey back to his own country, where he will encounter the brother who swore to kill him. Twenty years earlier he had cheated his brother Esau out of the family blessing and inheritance. Twenty years earlier he had run from his brother when his brother vowed to kill him for doing that. He had gone five hundred miles north. He had settled in with some relatives. Over the twenty years he had married, had children, and grown wealthy. He now has vast flocks and herds, and a huge labor force to take care of them. And now, after twenty years, God has told him to return to his own country. But the unknown question is—What kind of a reception will he get from his brother? Has Esau softened over the years and forgiven him, or is he still nursing his anger and wanting to carry out his revenge against him?

God had promised to protect him as he returned. God had promised to be with him, and to safely settle him in his own land where he would become a great nation. God had promised that he would retain his wealth, and his leadership position over his brother—that his fortune and his family and his prominence would be secure. But could he trust God to do that, or did he need to compromise and maneuver and take matters into his own hands to protect himself?

That's the question Jacob's struggling with as he heads south, coming from Harran toward Canaan. He's coming down through the hills on the eastern side of the Jordan River. He's approaching the Jabbok River, which feeds into the Jordan. He'll need to cross a shallow ford at the Jabbok, and then find another ford to cross the Jordan River into the land God has promised him. But he knows that when he crosses the Jabbok, he'll be entering the area Esau has settled in. He's certain his brother will have heard of his coming. And the question is—What kind of a reception will he get? Will his brother kill him, steal everything he has, force his wives and children to be slaves? Can he trust God to protect him from Esau, or should he compromise and scheme and take matters into his own hand to protect himself?

As he travels over the hills toward the inevitable encounter with Esau, God reveals to Jacob how absolute is his promise of protection. He lets Jacob see the incredible protective force that is accompanying him—an army that will overwhelm any danger and eliminate any threat. He lets Jacob see how irrevocably committed he is to protecting him. Jacob can fully trust him.

And through what we will read, God will give you and me a brief glimpse of how we too can absolutely trust him because of the incredible protection that moves with us through life. We do not need to scheme or maneuver or plot or compromise, because God has an invisible force that accompanies us and moves with us to keep us safe for his purposes.

God reveals this invisible force to Jacob early one morning after his father-in-law, Laban, leaves (Gen. 31:55). As others are breaking camp to resume their journey through the hills to the Jabbok River, Jacob goes off by himself to look at the route ahead of them. He looks down the valleys and hills that they will traverse.

And all of a sudden, it's as though someone blinked something away from his eyes, and he sees an incredible army, more than he can count—rank upon rank, division upon division—all around him, ready to move through the hills ahead of them. An army of light. It's as though all the stars of night had come to earth in the early dawn, and gathered themselves into formation, ready to move like a river through the hills and valleys ahead of them. It's the angelic army of God, there to protect him and take him home.

> *Jacob also went on his way, and the angels of God met him. When Jacob saw them, he said, "This is the camp of God!" So he named that place Mahanaim. (Gen. 32:1–2)*

Something is removed from Jacob's eyes, and he sees the vast army of God. He names the place *Mahanaim*, which means "two camps." Two camps are there. Jacob's camp is breaking ground. But God's army camp is also there, ready to move out. Two camps—his camp and God's camp. And God's camp will move ahead to protect him.

You and I find it difficult to believe in this camp around us, because we don't see it. We have trouble believing in this angelic army ready to protect us, because it's invisible to us. The same was true in biblical times; they didn't believe in it either, because they hardly ever saw it. Only on rare occasions, when God would blink something from their eyes, would they suddenly see it.

Once, during the time of Elisha, when the hostile forces of Syria surrounded the city he was living in, and were ready to attack, Elisha's servant was terrified. And Elisha asked God to let him see the invisible angelic army that was in place.

> *When the servant of the man of God got up and went out early the next morning, an army with horses and chariots had surrounded the city. "Oh no, my lord, what shall we do?" the servant asked.*
>
> *"Don't be afraid," the prophet answered. "Those who are with us are more than those who are with them."*
>
> *And Elisha prayed, "Open his eyes, Lord, so that he may see." Then the Lord opened the servant's eyes, and he looked and saw the hills full of horses and chariots of fire all around Elisha. (2 Kings 6:15–17)*

An angelic army in place, ready to protect them against the Syrian forces.

Most of the time something covers our eyes so that we cannot see this angelic army ready to carry out God's purposes for us. But it's always in place, ready to move as God directs. We read in Psalms:

> This poor man called, and the Lord heard him;
>   he saved him out of all his troubles.
> The angel of the Lord encamps around those who fear him,
>   and he delivers them. (Ps. 34:6–7)

And again:

> He will command his angels concerning you
>   to guard you in all your ways. (Ps. 91:11)

This invisible army is always there to serve God's purposes. Occasionally we hear stories from the mission field of how enemy attackers retreat when they suddenly see this protective force.

It is not always God's intent that they act. It's not always his purpose that they insert themselves in our affairs. Jesus knew he could call on this invisible army, but he also knew it was not God's intent that they act in his situation. When Peter tried to defend him against the arresting soldiers that came in the Garden of Gethsemane, Jesus told Peter to put up his sword:

> "Put your sword back in its place," Jesus said to him, "for all who draw the sword will die by the sword. Do you think I cannot call on my Father, and he will at once put at my disposal more than twelve legions of angels? But how then would the Scriptures be fulfilled that say it must happen in this way?" (Matt. 26:52–54)

The angelic army was there, available, but God's purposes and the Scriptures required that they not act in his situation.

But we know that God's army is always in place around us, and that in potentially fearful or threatening situations we are to trust him rather than compromise and take matters into our own hands. We don't need to scheme or maneuver. We can trust God's invisible force to bring about his will.

Will Jacob do that? Will he trust God's promise to be with him, and to settle him back safely into his land? Will he trust God's promise that his family and fortune and place of prominence in the family—his leadership over his brother—will remain secure? Will he trust God to protect him from Esau, or will he take matters into his own hands?

Jacob blinks again, and now something is covering his eyes once more. He no longer sees the angelic army ready to move through the hills ahead of him. Instead, he sees the Jabbok River in the distance, and knows that on the other side he will encounter Esau, and he doesn't know what his brother will do.

What should he do? Should he take matters into his own hands? Should he try and cover his bases? Should he come up with some scheme or plan to protect himself? Or can he trust God to take care of him?

His fear and his anxiety win out. He comes up with his own scheme. He'll compromise. He'll give the family leadership back to Esau if that's what it takes to survive, and if it will turn Esau from his anger. Rather than trust God's promise of protection and that the family blessing will remain with him, he'll offer it back to Esau in exchange for safety.

And so he sends messengers to Esau, putting himself in the subservient position. Esau will be the lord; he will be Esau's servant. And he will give Esau whatever amount of money he wants to spare his life.

> Jacob sent messengers ahead of him to his brother Esau in the land of Seir, the country of Edom. He instructed them: "This is what you are to say to my lord Esau: 'Your servant Jacob says, I have been staying with Laban and have remained there till now. I have cattle and donkeys, sheep and goats, male and female servants. Now I am sending this message to my lord, that I may find favor in your eyes.'" (Gen. 32:3–5)

"Esau, I'm willing to take the subordinate, servant position. And I can offer you whatever you want—I have cattle, donkeys, sheep, goats. I have a huge labor force of male and female workers. Tell me what you want. I want to find favor in your eyes. I want you to spare me."

The messengers deliver the message and return. "What was Esau's response?" "He didn't say anything. All we know is that he gave orders for four hundred armed men to join him, and he's headed this way."

When the messengers returned to Jacob, they said, "We went to your brother Esau, and now he is coming to meet you, and four hundred men are with him." (Gen. 32:6)

What will Esau do? What are his intentions with these four hundred men? To give Jacob a royal welcome? To add his protection as Jacob returns home? Or to wipe him out, kill his family, and take his wealth?

Jacob cannot trust God to take care of him. His fear and distress have taken over. It's all up to him. He takes matters further into his own hands. He maneuvers, plots, and schemes. He devises his own plans to survive. He puts half his family in one group, and half in another. Half the flocks and herds go with one group, and half with another. If Esau attacks and wipes out one group, Jacob can still survive with the other.

In great fear and distress Jacob divided the people who were with him into two groups [literally, "two camps"], and the flocks and herds and camels as well. He thought, "If Esau comes and attacks one group [camp], the group [camp] that is left may escape." (Gen. 32:7–8)

And now, again, there are two camps. But now instead of it being Jacob's camp and God's camp, it's now the two camps of Jacob's fear and compromise and scheming. Jacob is no longer trusting God's camp, the angelic army. Instead he's counting on his plan to have two camps of his own. If Esau takes out one of them, perhaps the other will survive. Maybe this way he can hang on to half his family and his wealth.

He begs God to help him, but he has no confidence that he will. As far as Jacob is concerned, everything is going to depend on what he can do to protect himself. He desperately reminds God of his promises:

Then Jacob prayed, "O God of my father Abraham, God of my father Isaac, Lord, you who said to me, 'Go back to your country and your relatives, and I will make you prosper,' I am unworthy of all the kindness and faithfulness you have shown your servant. I had only my staff when I crossed this Jordan, but now I have become two camps. Save me, I pray, from the hand of my brother Esau, for I am afraid he will come and

attack me, and also the mothers with their children. But you have said,
"I will surely make you prosper and will make your descendants like the
sand of the sea, which cannot be counted." (Gen. 32:9-12)

He desperately reminds God of his promises. But when the morning comes, he fully takes matters into his own hands. He sends an incredible amount of wealth ahead to his brother, to buy him off. Wave after wave—huge herds of male and female animals, capable of breeding vast flocks. And he instructs his workers to again state his willingness to be subservient to Esau. Esau will be his lord, and he will be Esau's servant.

> *He spent the night there, and from what he had with him he selected*
> *a gift for his brother Esau: two hundred female goats and twenty male*
> *goats, two hundred ewes and twenty rams, thirty female camels with*
> *their young, forty cows and ten bulls, and twenty female donkeys and*
> *ten male donkeys. He put them in the care of his servants, each herd by*
> *itself, and said to his servants, "Go ahead of me, and keep some space*
> *between the herds."*
>
> *He instructed the one in the lead: "When my brother Esau meets*
> *you and asks, 'Who do you belong to, and where are you going, and*
> *who owns all these animals in front of you?' then you are to say, 'They*
> *belong to your servant Jacob. They are a gift sent to my lord Esau, and*
> *he is coming behind us.'"*
>
> *He also instructed the second, the third and all the others who*
> *followed the herds: "You are to say the same thing to Esau when you*
> *meet him. And be sure to say, 'Your servant Jacob is coming behind*
> *us.'" For he thought, "I will pacify him with these gifts I am sending*
> *on ahead; later, when I see him, perhaps he will receive me." So Jacob's*
> *gifts went on ahead of him, but he himself spent the night in the camp.*
> (Gen. 32:13–21)

And so the account sadly ends with another two camps. We've moved from the two camps of God and Jacob to the two camps of Jacob's scheming and maneuvering to the two camps of Jacob and Esau—Jacob alone in his camp, awaiting the coming camp of Esau.

Jacob has totally lost sight of God's camp. He cannot trust God to protect him. He's taken matters into his own hands. His schemes and gifts and bribes have now left him alone and anxious in his camp, fearing the arrival the next day of Esau with his camp of four hundred armed men.

And that night, alone and desperate, he will wrestle with God as never before—which we will see in the next section.

God's great appeal to you is to trust him. Though there's a covering over your eyes that keeps you from seeing, you can trust him—he has an overwhelming force standing by, ready to serve you as he directs.

You don't need to compromise in your dating or your work or your finances. You don't need to scheme or plot or take matters into your own hands. You can trust yourself into his protective care. He will bring the outcome he desires.

14

THE MAGNIFICENT DEFEAT

Genesis 32:22–32

When I was in my mid-twenties, I tried to preach the passage of Scripture that we're going to look at. But I couldn't preach it. Because at the time I didn't understand Jacob, I didn't understand God, and I didn't understand myself.

I was twenty-five years old. It was a summer during my years in seminary. My wife Nell and I were doing a summer internship at the Peninsula Bible Church in Palo Alto, California. In addition to working with the church's youth, I was going to have a chance to preach once in big church—the main service on Sunday morning.

About a month before my Sunday to preach, I started thinking about what I would preach on. And I decided to preach this passage. I thought: "Man, there's got to be a great message in here somewhere. God himself wrestles with Jacob all night long, changes his name, and leaves him a cripple. There's got to be great sermon in here somewhere—a sermon that will wow the people, knock their socks off, and make them say, 'Hey, who is that young preacher? He's good. Keep your eye on that young man—he's got a future!'" You can hear the ego in that.

So I started to work on the passage to make this great sermon. But the more I worked with it, the more confused and frustrated I got. I had no clue what was going on in the passage. I had nothing but questions:

Out of nowhere, a "man" suddenly attacks Jacob, and starts wrestling with him. Who is this man, and where does he come from?

As the story goes on, it becomes clear that it's not a man; it's really God who is wrestling with Jacob. But why? Why is God wrestling with him? And why can't God win? Why can't God overpower him? They go at it in the darkness, without a word, for hours, furiously trying to break each other, trying to get a hold on the other that would make them give up. And Jacob holds his own until God, after hours of being unable to subdue Jacob, finally zaps him in the leg—seems like dirty pool; Jacob doesn't have one of those zappers. God zaps him so that he can get away from Jacob before the sun comes up.

But then Jacob won't let him go. Here he's been fighting this attacker for hours to protect himself, and now that the attacker is finally willing to leave him alone, Jacob won't let him get away. Busted hip and all, he hangs on to the one who's been trying to hurt him all night.

And then God asks Jacob what his name is. Why does God have to ask Jacob what his name is? Whom does he think he's been wrestling with all night?

Then God says, "Jacob, you've won, you've overcome," and he changes Jacob's name. Jacob didn't win. He was crippled. He limped for the rest of his life. Why does God say he won? And why change his name?

And then, when Jacob very politely asks, "Tell me your name also. We've talked about my name; can you tell me yours?" But God won't tell him. Why not?

Nothing but questions.

I worked and worked on the passage for about a week and a half, trying to make some sense out of it. And I finally gave up. I had no idea what was going on in it. I don't remember what sermon I eventually preached when my Sunday came, but whatever it was, the congregation never got the benefit of the glorious one I was planning.

I was twenty-five, I didn't understand Jacob, I didn't understand God, and I didn't understand myself.

As the years have passed, I think I have a little better understanding of God and of myself, and as a result, as I come to this passage again, I think I have a little better understanding of Jacob.

What's going on in this passage? What's happening to Jacob? What's the point here? What is it that God wants us to focus on, in order to understand how he works in our lives?

The point, my friend, is this: This is the moment when God forever breaks us, and sets us on a path of blessing. This is the defining moment, when the issue is settled between us and God—is it going to be his way or our way? What I want or what God wants?

In my marriage, in my job, in my career, with my children—am I going to do things the way God wants, or is it going to be the way I want? This is the defining moment—the moment we are broken.

Until God breaks us, we resist and struggle. We fight for all we're worth, and refuse to give in. But finally, at some point, God's says, "That's enough." God breaks us. He wins. But then we discover, "We are the winners!" We've overcome! Our defeat . . . has brought us victory!

This is the defining moment in life when you know that you have been defeated by God, and, as a result, your life is forever blessed. It's a magnificent defeat.

This defining moment comes out of nowhere. You're not expecting it. You're preoccupied with other things. Your attention is elsewhere. And when the moment hits, you say to yourself, "Whoa, where did this come from? What's going on? What's happening to me?" And it takes you a while to figure it out.

Jacob isn't expecting this attack. His attention has been on other things. His mind has been preoccupied with what was going to happen the next day.

The next day he's going to cross the border river back into his own land for the first time in twenty years. He's heard that his brother Esau has gotten wind of his return and is heading to the river from the other side with an army of about four hundred armed men. And Jacob fears that as soon as he crosses the river, Esau will massacre him, his family, his herdsmen, and all of his other servants.

Why does he expect to be massacred by his own brother? Because twenty years earlier he had cheated his brother out of the family inheritance. He had tricked their blind father Isaac into making him the head of the clan and giving him the family blessing instead of his older brother. He had stolen the birthright. When Esau had discovered this, he had vowed to kill Jacob. And so twenty years earlier Jacob had fled to save his life.

He left in a hurry, penniless, with nothing. He set out for a distant land, hoping to find some relatives and stay with them. After traveling for hundreds of miles, he managed to find the relatives. He settled in with them and, over the years, married and had children. Over the twenty years he had also become a wealthy man. Through some deceptive maneuvering, some astute business practices, and some plain old hard work, he managed to accumulate vast holdings of goats, sheep, cattle, donkeys, and even camels.

But his old habits of trickery, deceit, and manipulation eventually turned those relatives against him also. And so once again he had to leave in a hurry. He headed back to his own land, hoping that maybe after twenty years Esau might have softened a bit.

As he got closer to the border, he sent messengers to Esau to let him know he was coming back. He told his messengers, "See if you can get a reading on how Esau feels toward me after these twenty years." When his messengers returned, they said Esau's only response to the news was to assemble four hundred armed men, and that Esau and his army were only a day behind them, nearing the border from the other side

And Jacob's mind is entirely preoccupied with what's going to happen next. How can he make it through tomorrow? What can he do to get around Esau—to out-maneuver him again, to finesse the situation to his advantage? What can he do to minimize the damage so that he can get back in the land and get on with his life? All of his attention, all of his thinking, all of his calculations are focused on the expected clash with Esau the next day.

He's come up with a plan he thinks will work. Jacob always has a plan. He's always got a scheme. His plan is to divide his huge caravan into two groups and send them across the river at two widely separated spots. He himself will stay on this side of the river. Then, if Esau finds one of the groups and massacres it, he'll think he's wiped out Jacob and he'll leave and go home. And then Jacob will join the other group, and with at least one-half of his family and wealth, he'll go find some place to survive.

And then he gets another idea—maybe he can prevent a massacre, maybe he could buy Esau off with some gifts. And so he sends ahead a huge flock of goats—220, bawling and scampering all over the place—with instructions to his shepherds, "If you come across my brother Esau, and he asks you, 'Who are you guys, where are you going, and whose animals are these?' tell him, 'They're Jacob's, and he wants you to have them; he's willing to make up for what he's done.'" And so the shepherds and 220 goats take off.

Then, when he thinks the goats have probably traveled half a mile, he sends shepherds with 220 sheep milling around, bumping into each other, and these shepherds carry the same message, "These sheep are Jacob's gift to you. He's willing to do anything you want."

Then, a little while later, he sends camels. After that, cows and bulls. Then donkeys. Wave after wave of expensive gifts are started on their way, hopefully to wear Esau down and bring him around. Lots of ideas, lots of plans, lots of schemes to solve his problem.

As night falls, Jacob supervises the river crossing of his family, his vast herds, and all his possessions—the two groups that will head for separate spots across the border. After they leave, he's by himself, lost in thought, wondering if there's anything else he could do to salvage the situation. Has he done enough? Is there anything else he could try?

And while he's alone, preoccupied, focused on other things, thinking and pondering and scheming, out of nowhere, out of the darkness, an assassin leaps on him, puts a stranglehold on him and begins to choke the life out of him. And suddenly, unexpectedly, Jacob finds himself in a wrestling match that will go on for hours—a defining moment that will determine whether he lives or dies.

> That night Jacob got up and took his two wives, his two female servants and his eleven sons and crossed the ford of the Jabbok. After he had sent them across the stream, he sent over all his possessions. So Jacob was left alone, and a man wrestled with him till daybreak. (Gen. 32:22–24)

Suddenly, out of nowhere, a man leaps on him, in order to destroy him.

My friend, your defining moment will come just as unexpectedly, out of nowhere. It did for me. Ten years after that egotistical Palo Alto summer I was a young pastor in Scottsdale, Arizona. I had been pastoring Scottsdale

Bible Church for two to three years. There had been a spurt of growth when I first came, but attendance had leveled off. Then it began to decline.

As the attendance continued to drop, I became concerned. My thoughts and attention were drawn to the problem. I became preoccupied with it. "This is not good," I said to myself, "this drop in attendance." I had grown up in a church of several thousand, and I wanted to pastor a big church like that, but we were getting smaller, not bigger. I had won the graduating award at seminary for the student who best represented the ideals of the seminary, the student most likely to succeed. But this was not success. I was hoping to teach at the seminary some day—to teach others how to pastor and preach. But who wants a professor who couldn't successfully do it himself? The Christian magazines don't run too many articles on "I went to a church of five hundred and under my leadership it became a church of one hundred." How could I make a name for myself if the church didn't grow?

And I became preoccupied with fixing the problem. What could we do to reverse the trend? What kind of sermons could I preach to make people want to come? What could we change around here to make it better? Let's think, let's plan, let's ponder.

But instead of getting better, it got worse. The decline became more dramatic. The attendance line on the graph was going down and showed no sign of bottoming out. Nothing I did seemed to help. I didn't know any way to stop the decline. The church seemed to be dying.

I remembered Winston Churchill's words during World War II—"I have not been called to preside over the dissolution of the British Empire"—and I was afraid I *had* been called to preside over the dissolution of Scottsdale Bible Church.

What would that do to me? To my self-image as someone who succeeds? What would that do to my future plans to teach at the seminary? If the church died, how would I survive and stay intact emotionally? If I killed this church, no one would ever call me to pastor another one.

And suddenly, without knowing where it had come from, I found myself in a defining moment, wrestling with a situation where my soul would either live or die.

My friend, that defining moment in your life comes unexpectedly, out of nowhere. At first it starts out as a nagging problem. It may be a nagging difficulty in your marriage—some irritation, some troublesome issue, stupid arguments that go on for days, different ideas on how to handle work schedules, in-laws, or finances.

It may be at work. It may begin with a downturn in the business, accounts going elsewhere, clients not reordering, or employees going to work for a competitor.

It may be in your career. Someone else gets the promotion you thought you were up for, and you suddenly realize you're stalled in your advancement; you're not on the fast track any more. Work has become repetitive and unsatisfying, and you're tired of the people you have to see every day.

The defining moment may emerge through your children. They're having problems in school. Behavioral problems—lack of attention in class, fights during recess, disrespect to teachers. Academic problems—no interest in schoolwork, poor grades. Social problems—hanging around with the wrong crowd, dating undesirable people.

And you're thinking about these nagging problems—these problems in your marriage, at work, with your career, or with your kids. You're thinking about these problems—"What can I do to solve them? How can I get past them? How can I handle them? What if I do this? What if I say that? Maybe I should . . ." And you're preoccupied with how you're going to handle them, how you're going to maneuver things to make it all work.

But then suddenly, without warning, everything blows up in your face. What started out as a nagging problem all of a sudden mushrooms into a fearful catastrophe. What began as a difficulty that needed a solution has become a disaster that is heading to destruction.

Now, all of a sudden, the marriage is seriously falling apart. You're hardly speaking to each other any more. You hate going home. Sometimes the anger is so great one of you goes to a motel or stays with a friend.

Or at work, things are disintegrating. Red ink is piling up. There's every possibility the downsizing will include you, and finding another job in your field will be almost impossible.

Your child stays out all night and you don't know where. He's getting in trouble with the law, becoming physically abusive to others in the family, showing signs of addiction.

And you suddenly find yourself in a life-or-death struggle—everything is falling apart. You don't know whether you'll live or die. In shock and horror, you ask, "What's happening? What's going on? Where did this come from?"

It takes you a while to realize it comes from God. It takes you a while to realize it's not your spouse, it's not your boss, it's not your job, it's not your child. It's God, and you.

It's God who has leaped into your circumstances. It's God who has assailed your life. It's God struggling with you to remove something from your life—to break you of pride, to remove your self-centeredness, your love-lessness. It's God, grappling with you to turn you from impurity and pornography. It's God, trying to grab you from the pursuit of money. It's God, wrapping himself around you, breathing on you, in your face, demanding to be central in your life, demanding that you look at him . . . and yield.

It takes us a while to realize it's God. And that's why the struggle goes on so long and never seems to end. We're stubborn. We point to something else or someone else. We don't see the real issue, and so the struggle goes on and on, because we don't realize it's God.

When the attack came on Jacob, he didn't think it was God. He thought it was a man—a human enemy, an assassin, a bandit. Or maybe one of Esau's thugs sent to kill him. He didn't know it was God. He thought it was a man. And so the struggle went on and on, for hours.

> So Jacob was left alone, and a man wrestled with him till daybreak [for four, six, eight hours]. (Gen. 32:24)

The reason it went on so long was because Jacob wasn't going to let this man beat him. Jacob fought him for hours, for all he was worth. Jacob had always been physically strong, able to lift a stone over a well that normally took four people to lift. He'd always been able to hold his own. And he would handle this moment too. He would beat this man. He would force the situation to bend to his will. All his life he had been tough and smart and had gotten the best of everyone and everything, and he would win again.

But the man cannot be beaten. His strength matches Jacob's. In fact, there seems to be some hidden power in the man that scares Jacob, causing him to struggle more furiously and frantically to keep the man from over-powering him. On and on through the night, the man presses and presses, looking for the death hold, and Jacob in desperation beats back every move.

Until the moment comes when the man reveals who he really is and that he's been holding back all along, that he has the strength and the power to break him at any moment. The man simply touches Jacob with an energy or force he's not previously used, and Jacob's hip is broken forever.

When the man saw that he could not overpower him, he touched the socket of Jacob's hip so that his hip was wrenched as he wrestled with the man. (Gen. 32:25)

At some point we, like Jacob, come face to face with the raw presence of God. At some point in our struggle, our stubbornness, our resistance, our pride, our rebellion—at some point God says, "That's enough," and we are forever broken before him.

That's what happens to Jacob. God zaps him and says, "Jacob, that's enough. All your life you've been unwilling to let me be in control. I've promised you good. I've told you of my plans, what I'll do for you. But you've never waited for me to do it. You've never believed that I would do what I said. You've never trusted me to do it. You've gone off on your own, doing it your way, counting on your own schemes, your own cleverness, your own ability to handle things—cheating your brother, deceiving your father, alienating yourself from your father-in-law, and now manipulating your family into two groups, with bribes to Esau.

"You've never simply trusted me, depended on me. Now, as I promised, you're about to come back into the land. After twenty years you're returning to the place where all of my destiny for you will take place, where I will make your children into a great nation. And even though I'm bringing you back as I promised, you're still depending on your own wits and cleverness, you're still trying to finesse the situation, you're still trying to maneuver around

Esau—dividing your family into two groups, to save your own skin. You're still not trusting me, depending on me, relying on me, looking to me. Jacob, that's enough; it cannot go on this way. You will yield." And God breaks him forever.

To a young pastor in Scottsdale, Arizona, God said, "Don, you've always had such a high, egotistical view of yourself; you've always thought you would succeed because of your abilities; you always assumed you could make anything happen. You've had your dreams and your ambitions—big church, famous name, prominent professor. And everything in your life has been focused on your pride. Don, that's enough. Now, as the attendance decline continues despite everything you try to do, you see that it's really all in my power, not yours. Now you see that regardless of who you are or what you do, this church is in my hand, for good or ill, not yours.

"This is the defining moment, Don. Do you serve me or yourself, my purpose or your pride? If I kill the church, will you still serve me? If I bury you so that no one ever hears of you again and all your ambitions and dreams die, will you still serve me? This is the moment of truth—do you serve me or your pride?"

And that moment, as I stared at the death of everything I wanted, the answer at that defining moment was, "I serve you. Do what you will, I will serve you. I will be a kernel of wheat and fall into the ground and die—if that's what you want.

"But God, can I at least hang on to one redeeming thought—that if the church dies, it's because you wanted it and not necessarily because I killed it? Can I at least kind of limp away from the disaster with a small shred of self-image still intact? Can I say it was because you wanted it to fail? Can I kind of be like Jeremiah—you told him you had called him to uproot, to tear down, to destroy (Jer. 1:10); you 'appointed' him to do that. I'm willing to serve you, and to stay and bury the church, but if it fails can I at least say you 'appointed' me to it, that it was your plan for my life. Can I give you the blame?"

And God said, "Yes. If it fails, I get the blame. And Don . . . if it succeeds, do I get the credit?"

Yes . . . Yes! And from that moment I was free. Free from worrying about myself, my future, my dreams. Forever broken, but free. Defeated, magnificently defeated, but forever blessed. The church may or may not die—that's for God to decide. But I'm free, released from it.

"It's not me, God, it's you. It's not my failure, and it's not my success. It's yours. It's not my skills, not my ability. It's whatever your intentions are. If you slay me, I will trust you. If you reward me, it will be your mercy. It's not me, it's you."

And from that defining moment has flowed the direction of my life. The attendance at the church continued to drop for a few months, but then it bottomed out and began to climb. But that was immaterial. At that defining moment the issue had been settled—it was going to be God, not me.

For Jacob also, the issue is settled. Broken, in great pain, no longer fighting, just desperately clutching, he says to God, "I know who you are and I will not let you go unless you bless me. You have crippled me, lamed me, taken away my strength. From now on I have no choice but to depend on you. I have to lean on you. But can I limp away from this defeat with a blessing?"

> Then the man said, "Let me go, for it is daybreak." But Jacob replied, "I will not let you go unless you bless me." The man asked him, "What is your name?" "Jacob," he answered. (Gen. 32:26–27)

When God says to him, "What is your name?" he's not asking for information. He's asking for an admission, a confession. He's asking for an acknowledgement: "What kind of man are you?"

In biblical times, a man's name described his character; it revealed his personality; it told you what kind of man he was. "What is your name? Be honest with me—what are you like?"

"My name is . . . Jacob"—in Hebrew that means "heel-grabber." Because when Jacob and his twin brother Esau were born, Esau came out first, but Jacob's small hand was grabbing his brother's heel, as though he wanted to pull him back into the womb and have himself be born first, so that he would be the one to carry on the family name. From the moment of birth and all through his life, he's been a grabber.

"My name is Jacob—heel-grabber, schemer, shrewd, smart operator, con-man, hustler, manipulator. I am 'Jacob.' All my life I've been 'Jacob.' I've always been a self-centered, scheming 'Jacob.' My name is Jacob. God, that's what I am—Jacob."

Broken, forever defeated. But now comes the blessing.

"Your name will no more be 'Jacob.' I have now changed you, and you will forever be different. I have changed you and now I change your name. I have changed your character, and now I change your identity."

> Then the man said, "Your name will no longer be Jacob, but Israel, be-
> cause you have struggled with God and with humans and have over-
> come." (Gen. 32:28)

"Your name will be 'Israel.'" *Israel* in Hebrew means "He struggles with God." "You have struggled with God, and you have come out ahead. You have won the larger battle, the battle over yourself. You have prevailed in the real issue, the issue of your pride and self-reliance. You have struggled with God, and though magnificently defeated, you have overcome that old prideful, scheming, egotistical self, and you are blessed. You will be forever different."

Before Jacob lets go, he says, "Tell me your name. Who are you? How can I get a handle on you? How can I get ahold of you in the future? Whom do I call? What if I want you to do something for me in the future? What if there are things in the future that I want you to bless? What name do I call out to get you coming?"

> Jacob said, "Please tell me your name." But he replied, "Why do you ask
> my name?" Then he blessed him there. (Gen. 32:29)

"Why do you ask my name?" "Do you think you can have me at your beck and call in the future? That you can go back to making your own plans and then take me out of a box to do your bidding? Do you think that you can control me and put me at your disposal? It is enough that I bless you now. And in the future I will decide again whether I will bless you."

The man then disappears after the long night of struggle. As the sun rises, and as Jacob reflects on what happened, he calls the place *Peniel*, which in Hebrew means "face of God."

> *So Jacob called the place Peniel, saying, "It is because I saw God face to face, and yet my life was spared."*
>
> *The sun rose above him as he passed Peniel, and he was limping because of his hip. Therefore to this day the Israelites do not eat the tendon attached to the socket of the hip, because the socket of Jacob's hip was touched near the tendon.* (Gen. 32:30–32)

As Jacob walks to the border to cross the river, as Jacob walks into the future to meet his brother Esau, with every step he takes, he rises and falls—limping, sinking low on one hip—every step dramatically reminding him of that one defining moment, that magnificent defeat, when his life was forever changed, when God blessed him and made him different.

My friend, is God bringing you to a defining moment? In some area of your life—your marriage . . . your work . . . your children—some area where you've resisted, struggled, wrestled, trying everything you can think of, but you're still in some tight hold that you can't break out of. Is God bringing you to a moment when he's going to say, "That's enough! Is it me or you? My way or your way? Do you serve me or do you serve yourself?"

Let it be him. It's a magnificent defeat. And you are forever blessed.

15

LIKE SEEING THE FACE OF GOD

Genesis 33

When I was pastoring in Austin, Texas, there was a fine young man in the church who was very obviously waiting for God to bring him the right girl to marry. His name was David. He was a good-looking guy with a good job. As the years went by, we would see him at church with one girl or another who looked like she might be the one. But then, after a few months of dating, we wouldn't see her any more.

Finally, as he was moving into his middle thirties and beginning to wonder whether he'd ever get married, some friends put him together with a beautiful girl named Sonja, who lived a couple of hours away. She was also in her mid-thirties and she too had begun to wonder if God had a special man for her. They immediately took to each other, and within a few months we were all gathering for a joyful wedding.

At the rehearsal dinner the night before the wedding, some of the groomsmen started teasing David about how many girls he had dated over the years. And David, with a big smile and an arm around a radiant Sonja standing beside him, said, "I just want to say how thankful I am that none of the other girlfriends worked out."

Most of us have had a similar feeling at one time or another. "Lord, I'm thankful you didn't take me in that direction, because the direction you did take me in is so much better. At the time, when you closed a door, I wondered what you were doing, but when I look back at the new door you opened up, I say, "You are a good and wonderful God.""

I had that experience when I finished my graduate studies at UCLA and was looking for my first church to pastor. I had two interviews with a church in Arcadia, California, the city right next to Pasadena, where I grew up and where my folks lived. They had scheduled a congregational meeting to vote on whether to call me as pastor. The chairman of the elder board told me he expected it to be a ninety-five percent positive vote, and that he was sure I would be their next pastor. I was excited—a good church, near my family! But at the congregational meeting, one of the members mentioned that another man whom they all knew had just recently become available as a pastor, and the folks at the meeting quickly discarded me and began to pursue him. And I said, "God, what are you doing? That was a good church, close to my family. What happened?"

Following that, over the next six to eight months, I interviewed with another four or five churches around the country, but they too all turned me down. One door after another was closing.

And then a church in Irving, Texas, contacted me. This was the church Nell and I had attended while I was a student at the seminary. This was the church where I had been the unofficial youth pastor, and had then started a couples' Sunday school class, which had mushroomed in size. This was the church where I had led the music at the worship service. "Okay, Lord, now I understand. No wonder all the previous doors had closed! You were saving me for this one!" This church knew me, and I knew them. Not only that, the church was just a half-hour away from the seminary, so I could also do some teaching at the seminary while I was pastoring. "Good thinking, Lord. Thank you! This is going to work out great!"

But it didn't work out. There were several long-distance phone calls between me in California and the church committee members in Texas. They were concerned that maybe my graduate studies in communication had changed the way I would preach. The phone calls were so frustrating. I couldn't convince them that my views about preaching were still the same. Eventually, that church too joined the long list of churches that had turned me down. Another door closed. "God, what are you doing? That one was perfect. My self-image is taking a terrible beating. Does anybody want me?"

A couple of months later a church in Scottsdale, Arizona, near Phoenix, asked if I would just come for just one Sunday as a pulpit supply—a guest preacher. The pastoral search group had been going through the process of looking for a pastor and had narrowed their list of candidates to two or three that they were quite serious about. But they needed someone to preach on a particular Sunday, and I had been suggested. I flew over and preached. The people were very responsive. After the service, one of the leading ladies of the church came up to me and said, "How can we get you?" I mumbled something about "I assume there was a committee or something that she could talk to." And then I flew back to California.

I found out later that when the pastoral search group met over the next couple of days, they quickly set aside the list of men they were looking at and said, "Let's talk about this guy who preached for us last Sunday." And that was the beginning of exactly what God had in mind for us. Within a month, Nell and I flew over for official interviews, and a few months later I was voted on and accepted. Nell and I were there for seven years—seven years that marvelously shaped us and launched us on the path that our lives have taken ever since.

That's the wonderful goodness of our God—closing doors until he opens the one he wants you to walk through. When he closes one chapter of your life, he's already written the pages of the next chapter, and they're so good, you can't wait to keep reading.

This is what Jacob discovers—that as God closes one door and moves him in a different direction, even though he's uncertain and afraid of what might be ahead, God has already gone down the path and is opening the door he wants him to enter.

He's returning to his own country for the first time in twenty years. Twenty years earlier he had fled to get away from his brother Esau. He had stolen the family blessing—the spiritual inheritance—from Esau. He had tricked their blind father Isaac into giving him the blessing instead of Esau, who as the oldest son was entitled to it. And Esau had vowed to kill him.

As he was fleeing, on his last night in the land, before he crossed the border, he had a dream—a dream of a staircase connecting heaven and earth. The angels of God were going up and down the staircase, moving out to do God's work on earth and returning. And in the dream, God himself appeared at the top of the staircase and said, "Jacob, I'll watch over you, and bring you safely back. I'm yet going to fulfill my promises to you to give you this land."

When Jacob woke from the dream, before he crossed the border to go north, he made a vow: If God would bring him back safely to his own land, then he, Jacob, would worship him and serve him forever.

> *If God will be with me and will watch over me on this journey I am taking and will give me food to eat and clothes to wear so that I return safely to my father's household, then the Lord will be my God.* (Gen. 28:20b–21)

Now he's returning to his own country. God has clearly closed the door behind him. His father-in-law, Laban, who once had welcomed and valued him, had turned against him.

> *Jacob noticed that Laban's attitude* [literally, "face"] *toward him was not what it had been. Then the Lord said to Jacob, "Go back to the land of your fathers and to your relatives, and I will be with you."* (Gen. 31:2–3)

In the original Hebrew of the Old Testament, the word *attitude* is literally the word for *face*. Jacob noticed that Laban's "face" was no long smiling toward him, but had instead turned into a dark frown.

This word *face* is going to become an important, conspicuous word as we continue through this section of Scripture. In our English translation, it will show up in different ways, as different words. But I'll note when it's the same word *face* in the original Hebrew. And we'll see that this word is being deliberately and repeatedly used to tie together what God is doing—closing one door and opening another.

God signals that he wants Jacob to go back to his own country by closing the door with Laban—the "face" of Laban was not what it had been.

We've all experienced this, in one way or another, where God just seems to close a door.

We're dating someone, having lots of fun. But at some point, we sense, "This isn't the one." There's nothing wrong with this person. But it's just not going anywhere. It's God's way of closing a door and saying, "Let me turn you in a different direction."

Or we're interested in going to a certain grad school. We know we've got a good enough GPA and are fully qualified, but for some reason we don't get accepted. God is closing a door.

Or our company relocates to another state. Our department gets phased out. Our best friend moves. Our last child leaves home. Someone dear to us dies. In one way or another, God is ending a chapter, asking us to turn in another direction.

And yet, as you and I turn in that new direction, we find ourselves a bit on edge, anxious, unsure. What's ahead? God has closed one door, but will he open another? What will happen? What will it be like? And sometimes we're even afraid to walk down that path.

Jacob was certainly afraid of what was ahead for him. Twenty years ago his brother had vowed that if he ever saw him again, he would kill him. Now Esau knew that he was coming back. Jacob had gotten word that his brother was on his way toward him with four hundred armed men.

To appease his brother, to buy his favor, Jacob had sent wave after wave of expensive gifts—hundreds of goats, then after half a mile, hundreds of sheep. Followed half a mile later by camels, then cows and bulls, then donkeys—all spaced out, all designed to soften Esau and make him favorable toward Jacob. Jacob's thinking was:

> *"I will pacify him with these gifts I am sending on ahead* ["from my face"]; *later, when I see him* ["his face"], *perhaps he will receive me* ["lift my face"]. *So Jacob's gifts went on ahead of him* ["from his face"], *but he himself spent the night in the camp.* (Gen. 32:20b–21)

The Hebrew word *face* is tying all these events together. Behind him the "face" of Laban was not what it was. God had closed that door. But now he wondered what would be the "face" of Esau ahead of him—whether God would open that door for him.

That night, before he crossed the border back into his land, a man leaped out of the darkness to kill him. Jacob thought it was an assassin sent by Esau. But as they wrestled and fought, hour after hour, Jacob realized this was no ordinary man. This was God, in human form, determined once and for all to break him. This was going to be a defining moment in Jacob's life, when God would forever break him of his scheming and deceiving and manipulating and maneuvering—a defining moment when Jacob would decide once and for all whether he would trust God, or whether he would continue to do things his way.

God broke him that night. God busted his hip. And then God changed his name to indicate the change that had taken place in his character. His name would no longer be Jacob—no longer heel-grabber, no longer con man, schemer, shrewd operator, manipulator. No longer Jacob. Now his name would be Israel—"Is-ra-el," one who has struggled with God and won the battle, one who has wrestled and overcome the real issue of pride and self-reliance.

When the long battle was over, when Jacob was broken, when his name was changed and God had blessed him, as the sun was rising and he got ready to limp ahead and join his family, Jacob named the place "the face of God."

> *Jacob called the place Peniel* ["the face of God"], *saying, "It is because I saw God face to face, and yet my life was spared."* (Gen. 32:30)

He has seen the face of God, and now he's ready to trust him as he moves toward the face of his brother. God has closed the door behind him. The face of Laban has turned against him. But the face of God has appeared to him. What will be the face of his brother? Will God open that door?

As our passage opens, the two brothers meet after twenty years:

> *Jacob looked up and there was Esau, coming with his four hundred men; so he divided the children among Leah, Rachel and the two female servants. He put the female servants and their children in front, Leah and her children next, and Rachel and Joseph in the rear. He himself went on ahead and bowed down to the ground seven times as he approached his brother.* (Gen. 33:1–3)

Bowing, and then getting up and moving forward, and bowing again was the standard way of showing honor to a dignitary. It was the protocol of the day, the way you approached some high official.

And Jacob discovers that God has opened the door! God has changed Esau's heart. Even as Jacob is bowing, Esau is running toward Jacob. And the two brothers embrace and weep.

> *But Esau ran to meet Jacob and embraced him; he threw his arms around his neck and kissed him. And they wept.* (Gen. 33:4)

The two brothers stand, hugging, kissing each other's necks, the tears flowing—it's been twenty years. Finally they separate, and Esau, looking at the women and children, asks, "Who are all these people with you? And what were all those animals that came on me in droves?"

> *Then Esau looked up and saw the women and children. "Who are these with you?" he asked.*
>
> *Jacob answered, "They are the children God has graciously given your servant."*
>
> *Then the female servants and their children approached and bowed down. Next, Leah and her children came and bowed down. Last of all came Joseph and Rachel, and they too bowed down.*
>
> *Esau asked, "What's the meaning of all those flocks and herds I met?"*
>
> *"To find favor in your eyes, my lord," he said.*
>
> *But Esau said, "I already have plenty, my brother. Keep what you have for yourself."* (Gen. 33:5–9)

But Jacob insists, because he has come from the face of God to the face of his brother, and both faces are full of love. He sees in the face of brother the same mercy and forgiveness he saw in the face of God.

> *"No, please!" said Jacob. "If I have found favor in your eyes, accept this gift from me. For to see your face is like seeing the face of God, now that you have received me favorably. Please accept the present that was brought to you, for God has been gracious to me and I have all I need."*
> *And because Jacob insisted, Esau accepted it.* (Gen. 33:10–11)

"God closed a door when the face of Laban turned against me. But when he broke me, I saw his face, and I knew he would open a door for me here. And now I see reflected in you the face of the God who has brought me safely home."

My friend, that's your God. When you see God's face and are convinced that he's for you, the face of the future is full of laughter and joy. A door behind you may have closed, but it's only because God is opening up one ahead of you.

The brothers part and go their separate ways. Esau tries to get Jacob to come with him, but Jacob pleads that his family and herds couldn't keep the pace that Esau and his four hundred men would set. Esau's men would be understandably anxious to get back to their homes, and wouldn't want to be held up by the slow pace of the small children and nursing animals in his group. Esau understands and offers to leave a few men as protection for Jacob, but Jacob says that's unnecessary. He really doesn't need anything else now that he's found favor in Esau's eyes.

> Then Esau said, "Let us be on our way; I'll accompany you."
>
> But Jacob said to him, "My lord knows that the children are tender and that I must care for the ewes and cows that are nursing their young. If they are driven hard just one day, all the animals will die. So let my lord go on ahead of his servant, while I move along slowly at the pace of the flocks and herds before me and the pace of the children, until I come to my lord in Seir."
>
> Esau said, "Then let me leave some of my men with you."
>
> "But why do that?" Jacob asked. "Just let me find favor in the eyes of my lord." (Gen. 33:12–15)

So the brothers separate. Esau heads toward his home. Jacob heads toward the Jordan River. He stops for several days before he crosses the river, to build shelters for his nursing animals. After they've regained their strength from the long journey, he crosses the river and makes his way to a place called Shechem where he purchases a large tract of land for his family.

So that day Esau started on his way back to Seir. Jacob, however, went to Sukkoth, where he built a place for himself and made shelters for his livestock. That is why the place is called Sukkoth.

After Jacob came from Paddan Aram, he arrived safely at the city of Shechem in Canaan and camped within sight of the city. For a hundred pieces of silver, he bought from the sons of Hamor, the [founding] father of Shechem, the plot of ground where he pitched his tent (Gen. 33:16–19)

He has *arrived safely* in the land. He's come to the special place of Shechem—the place where God had first promised Abraham that he would give this land to him and his family (12:6–7).

God has fulfilled his promises to Jacob—that he would watch over him, bring him safely back, and give the land to him (28:13–15). And now Jacob fulfills his vow to God:

If God will be with me and will watch over me on this journey I am taking and will give me food to eat and clothes to wear so that I return safely to my father's household, then the Lord will be my God. (Gen. 28:20–21)

The Lord will be the God of Jacob, now newly named Israel. And so, to fulfill his vow, Jacob sets up an altar and commits his life to the God who has loved him and been faithful to him:

After Jacob came from Paddan Aram, he arrived safely at the city of Shechem in Canaan. . . . There he set up an altar and called it El Elohe Israel [which means "God is the God of Israel"]. (Gen. 33:18–20)

My friend, when you see the face of God, when you see his love and his unchangeable goodness to you, when you know that his door to the future will lead to laughter and to joy, you gladly give him your life.